C000245895

an **otterton**mill
foodbook

2

## Introduction

*It's all about luck I guess, or good timing at least. When we arrived at Otterton Mill several years ago now we had no idea that it would become quite the institution that it has. Happily, our arrival coincided with a huge revival of interest in all things local, in opposition to the 'global' culture that was being foisted on us by those who had most to gain from reducing the world to a series of anonymous markets where every piece of artwork looked the same and every plate of food tasted similar.*

*To us the idea of selling sugar-packed soft drinks made under licence for a company based in the United States when we have far better, natural fruit juices available from Devon is quite absurd. Similarly, why pollute the environment by dragging sad-looking vegetables half way around the world when we have fantastic produce available locally? At the Mill we are proud to support Devon suppliers in our restaurant, our bakery, our shop and our gallery. We do this because Devon is a highly distinctive, vibrant county crammed full of talented, hard working, enthusiastic people who deserve our support and the support of our customers - and, unless you haven't guessed, because we love the place to bits.*

*At Otterton Mill we set out to create an environment where people could relax, enjoy top quality locally sourced food cooked to perfection, listen to great music and appreciate some of the finest contemporary artwork around. Alone or together, it should make no difference. In many ways it represents the culmination of everything that both of us have always tried to encourage during our varied careers; but more than that, the Mill is a place that we feel comfortable with and that we and our fabulous staff enjoy working in.*

*We hope that this book offers a similar experience. It's bursting with simple yet stimulating recipes, created by our superb team of chefs and bakers. But, and it's a big but, please don't take any of what follows too seriously. Even our chefs don't follow these recipes faithfully. They, like you, possess enquiring minds and the ability to experiment and adapt at will. Think of them as you might think of free-form jazz. We can provide a starting point and the rest is only limited by your imagination and sense of adventure. We wish you well.*

*Otterton Mill is a unique place and it is, therefore, appropriate that this book is unlike other cookbooks. For a start it isn't really a cookbook at all, more a kind of celebration of local culture. We interview several of our food producers with interesting stories to tell and we visit all corners of the region courtesy of our three generously gifted photographers. We also feature other elements of this extraordinary place such as our famous bakery, our craft gallery, our increasingly popular music venue and, of course, our watermill - our whole raison d'etre, after all. Enjoy.*

*Bob Butler and Claire Stein*

## The Mill in its landscape

*East Devon is beautiful. That's not merely a partisan assertion; it's official. Pretty much all of it is an Area of Outstanding Natural Beauty, and its extraordinary coastline (which, thanks to Steven Spielberg, we shall have to call 'The Jurassic Coast', even though it's actually Mesozoic) is the only natural World Heritage Site in England. Ours is a subtle, even secretive, landscape of long undulating hills with villages and hamlets tucked into their folds. Motorised transport has rotated the human geography. Traffic bustles through going east and west, to and from Exeter and Plymouth and the summer fleshpots of Torquay and St. Ives. But the natural geography of East Devon runs north and south. To see this plainly, we should take the buzzard's-eye view. From high above, it becomes clear that East Devon has ribs: a sequence of high heathland ridges that run down to the sea, where they end abruptly in great cliffs and turrets of red sandstone or white limestone. Between these ribs run our rivers: the Axe, the Sid, the Otter and, at our western limit, the Exe. Once, these were great land-gouging torrents fuelled by the melting of the ice-cap whose southern edge was a mere hundred miles north of here. Now they have dwindled, and wander - amiably, most of the time - through wide low alluvial valleys. For hundreds of years before the advent of the petrol engine these rivers were the arteries of East Devon's transport, trade, and business.*

*The Otter is a mischievous river. On its eastern bank, for much of its length, it's held in check by a low sandstone cliff. But it is constantly nibbling away at the opposite bank, stealing chunks of water meadow, toppling trees, changing its channels, sneaking gravel islets and silt beaches from one place to another. It is alive, and full of life. Squadrons of mullet browse where the water runs clear over gravel. Swans breed here, and if you are patient you will eventually glimpse that turquoise bullet, the kingfisher. Recently, egrets -snow white waders with lime-yellow socks - have taken up residence and vie for fishing rights with the native herons. Even far upriver, you may come upon the rather bizarre sight of cormorants perched high in trees. And in discreet places the animal that gave the river its name has been reintroduced after a long absence.*

*In the lagoons and channels of its estuary, the Otter provides a rich habitat for a great variety of indigenous birds and a way-station for flocks of migrants. It is a wonderful thing to stand here at sunset and listen to the music of the place; the fluting, bubbly calls of oystercatcher and curlew cut across by the brassy honking of an incoming flight of Brent geese. A sort of fanfare for the end of a river's journey.*

*All of East Devon's rivers had water-mills. Dozens of them. Now, Otterton Mill is the only one still functioning. In fact, it has been in almost continuous use for over a thousand years.*

4

In late Saxon times, the manor of Otterton belonged to King Harold's mother. Unsurprisingly, William the Conqueror did not let this state of affairs continue. He gave the Manor to the Norman Abbey of Mont St. Michel, who built a Priory here. (The original church tower and the chapter house remain.) For four centuries - until Henry V repossessed and sold the manor - the Brothers held sway over this large chunk of Devon, dominating its trade in milling, fishing, farming, woollen cloth and salt.

The mill has always been, and still is, the hub of its community. In its time it has also been a granary, a slaughterhouse, stabling for heavy horses, a cattle market, a haulier's and a turkey farm. It has evolved, changed shape, rearranged itself. The present buildings of warm, coarse, red sandstone date from the middle of the 19th century. But by the middle of the 20th century, Otterton Mill had fallen into disuse and disrepair. It was rescued and restored by Desna Greenhow and her alliance of enthusiasts and craftsmen, and in 1977, after a brief pause of twenty years, the millwheel turned again.
Under Desna's stewardship, the mill was lovingly resurrected as a museum, art gallery and restaurant. Now it is that, and more. Clare Stein and Bob Butler, with their passionate commitment to top-quality local produce, to local art and crafts, to music, have made the mill one of the most popular eating places in the county.

5

## A note on the recipes

*Great food can only come from great raw materials. It doesn't need to be fancy. Simple, fresh, local ingredients cooked with care are always fantastic. The ingredients are at least as important as the cook or the recipe.*
*So, in our recipes when we say chicken we mean free-range, organic, full-of-flavour chicken. When we say beef, pork, lamb, rabbit or venison we mean the best quality locally produced meat that you can buy.*
*Our eggs are fresh, local, free-range eggs, wonky and with bits of straw stuck to them if possible. We use lots of eggs laid by our own chickens (often amongst the plants we sell - look out for them). Our vegetables are fresh, organic where possible, locally produced and seasonal.*

*Many of the recipes use a mixture of precise weights -  8oz/225g and so on - as well as more relaxed measures like 'a handful' or 'a few sprigs' or even 'a little bit'. This is because although it is important to know the exact weights of the main ingredients, the recipes loosen up and allow cooks to use their taste buds and experiment a little.*
*The recipes in this book are not set in stone and cooking is not just about joining up the dots - adapt the recipes, enjoy cooking and, above all, enjoy eating.*

A book like this represents the combined effort of very many talented people. We should firstly thank Mal Peet and Elspeth Graham for the words, the editing and interviews. It's been a pleasure to work with them. As indeed it has with our photographers - Piers Rawson, Pauline Rook and Kimberly Rainford. We also need to thank Tony Weaver, whose design brief was not to design a cookbook at all, and James Crowden for his wise counsel in the early days. Charlie Money and Angie Briggs supplied additional photographs and Gilly Devon and Jane Osborne donated some of the original recipes. Clemmie Donald, Sue, Marjorie & Judy, the Harvey family, Denver, George, Chris & Dave (no, not Chas) and Steve Payne all helped with the photoshoots. Finally we need to thank all the suppliers who donated their valuable time and all our brilliant staff for reminding us just how lucky we are.

### January to December

The warm cows have gone
From the fields where the grass stands up
Dead-alive like steel.

Unexpected sun
Probes the house as if someone
Had left the lights on.

Novel no longer
Snowdrops melt in the hedge, drain
Away into spring.

The heron shining
Works his way up the bright air
Above the river.

Earth dries. The sow basks
Flat out with her blue-black young,
Ears over their eyes.

The early lambs, still
Fleecy, look bulkier now
Than their mothers.

In this valley, full
Of birdsong, the gap closes
Behind the cuckoo.

Fields of barley glimpsed
Through trees shine out like golden
Windows in winter.

Though nothing has changed -
The sun is even hotter -
Death is in the air.

Long shadows herald
Or dog every walker
In the cut-back lanes.

A crop of mist grows
Softly in the valley,
Lolls over the stawstacks.

Meadows filmed across
With rain stare up at winter
Hardening in the hills.

Patricia Beer

Patricia Beer
(1924-1999) was born in Exmouth and
spent the later part of her life in Upottery.
Her 'Collected Poems' are published by
Carcanet.

9

REVIVAL, RENEWAL AND REFURBISHMENT

CHRISTMAS & MILL DRESSING

PLANNING FOR THE YEAR AHEAD

COLD, STEAMY, INTIMATE AND RELAXED

SOUPS, SOUPS AND MORE SOUPS

TWINKLY LIGHTS AND COLD FROSTY MORNINGS

DUCKS IN THE COURTYARD

KINGFISHERS AND MOORHENS ON THE POND

SPECTACULAR EARLY SUNSETS

HOT CHOCOLATE, APPLE BRANDY AND SPICED MULLED WINE

WINTER

*At the time of the Doomsday Book, Otterton mill was one of the largest in Devon, grinding grain for this part of the lower Otter valley, and no doubt trading flour far beyond. It is listed as 'three mills'; that is, three sets of stones probably powered by a single wheel. By then, it - and the whole manor - was owned by the Benedictine Brotherhood of Mont St Michel. The monks of Otterton Priory baked bread for their own use, of course. They also distributed bread - most likely coarse barley bread - to the poor, and traded it for fish. The Prior had the right of first choice in the fish market. He also had the right to half of every dolphin landed and, furthermore, could claim every porpoise at the price of 'twelve pence and a loaf to each sailor, and two to the master'.*

Put all the dough ingredients in a bowl and stir them together until they form a soft dough. Remove the dough from the bowl and knead it for 5 minutes. Return it to bowl, cover and leave it until it's almost doubled in size - about 20 minutes.
Put the chopped dates in a pan with enough water to almost cover them. Heat gently and stir until they form a paste.
Add the other filling ingredients to the pan and allow them to melt together. Put to one side to cool a little.
Take the dough out of the bowl and knead it for a further 2 minutes. Return to the bowl to rest for another 5 minutes.
Then take the dough and roll it, on a lightly floured surface, into a square (the length of your loaf tin).
Cover the dough with the filling mix as evenly as possible. Then roll up the dough like a Swiss roll.
Oil the loaf tin. Tease the roll until it fits into the tin.
Finish off by pushing two hazelnuts into the top.

# DARK CHOCOLATE BREAD

Not one of our staple, traditional breads but a very popular sweet loaf to enjoy with a strong, frothy coffee on a cold winter's morning.

Leave in a warm, preferably humid place (this could be an airing cupboard), until the loaf has doubled in size.
Bake at 220°C/Gas mark 7 for about 20 minutes (light bake).
Remove from the tin at once, and put onto a cooling wire. (Baking should be so light that, if this is not done straightaway, sweating will occur, and then getting the loaf out of the tin will become more difficult).
Brush with some apricot jam mixed with a little hot water. When cool, dust with a little icing sugar.

THE DOUGH
1 lb/500g unbleached white flour
2oz/50g whole-wheat flour
2oz/50g fresh yeast
1oz/25g dark brown sugar
2 tablespoons of vegetable oil
2oz/50g black treacle
1oz/25g cocoa
1 level teaspoon of salt
1 egg
about 7 fl oz/200ml of warm milk

THE FILLING
1oz/25g cocoa
5oz/125g dark chocolate (70% cocoa solids)
5oz/125g chopped dates
1oz/25g toasted hazelnuts (keep a couple of nuts back to decorate)

13

BAKERY

# CULLEN SKINK

Cook the potatoes in lightly salted water.
Melt half the butter in a large heavy-based pan and add the leeks. Cook gently for about 10 minutes - until they are soft but not browned.
Drain the cooked potatoes (keep the cooking liquid) and mash them until they're smooth. Add the rest of the butter.
Whisk or blend together the mashed potatoes and the liquid they were cooked in. The texture should be smooth and creamy with the consistency of a thick soup. (Add some of the vegetable stock if necessary).
Stir into the leeks and bring gently to the boil. (Be warned that any soup with a lot of potatoes in will burn easily).
Skin and dice the smoked haddock, removing any obvious bones, and add to the simmering pan. Cook for a further few minutes until the fish is ready.
Stir in the cream and chives and check the seasoning. Serve.

Serves four to six

*i*

12oz/350g floury potatoes - peeled and cut into chunks
2oz/50g butter
4oz/125g leeks - finely chopped
1 lb/450g undyed smoked haddock
10 fl oz/300ml vegetable stock
sea salt and freshly ground black pepper
4 tablespoons of double cream
some chives - chopped

*This hearty smoked haddock, potato and leek soup was originally from the little fishing village of Cullen, in Scotland. The name means 'the essence of Cullen'. Sarah first came across this soup after a very cold winter day's riding with a friend. 'We arrived home to Cullen skink and crusty bread which my friend's husband had gone to lots of trouble to make - perfectly gorgeous!'*

15

FISH

# BEET SOUP WITH DILL & YOGURT

Pre-heat the oven to a hot setting. Scrub the beetroot, but leave them whole. Skin and quarter the onions. Put the vegetables in a roasting tin, cover them with the crushed garlic and drizzle them well with oil. Roast in the oven for about 30 minutes to an hour, until the skin can be easily peeled from the beetroot. Remove all from the oven and, when cool enough to handle, peel and chop the beetroot. Scrape all the contents of the roasting tin into a large saucepan and cover with vegetable stock, bring to the boil and simmer for 15 minutes. Blend until smooth and season to taste.
Reheat and serve with a spoonful of yogurt swirled on top and a good sprinkling of fresh dill.

This soup looks gorgeous - deep red with a white swirl and a sprinkling of green. Serves four.

*i*

1lb/450g raw beetroot
4 medium red onions
2 to 4 cloves of garlic, crushed
2 tablespoon of olive oil
2pts/1 litre vegetable stock
sea salt, freshly ground black pepper and lemon juice to season
some yogurt and a small handful of chopped fresh dill to serve

*Good soups are about good ingredients. A good soup can be made in minutes and be as tasty as one that takes an hour to prepare. Choose whether you want your soup chunky or smooth - or in-between. Vary ingredients and quantities to suit your taste.*

# CELERY, APPLE & CHESTNUT SOUP

Heat the oil and butter in a heavy-based pan and gently sauté the onion and celery for about 10 minutes until softened.

Add the cored and chopped apples and the chestnuts.

Cover with vegetable stock and simmer until all the ingredients are soft (about 20 minutes). Liquidise and adjust the consistency.

Season, adding lemon juice and maybe a pinch of sugar.

The soup will have a dull light brown colour but will taste rich, nutty and lightly sweet. Serve with a swirl of crème fraiche.

Ian invented this soup as the perfect accompaniment for his favourite cheese - Stilton.
A bowl of this, some fresh bread and a hunk of Stilton (or Devon Exmoor blue) on the side is, Ian promises, sublime.
Serves four to six

2 onions, peeled and chopped
1 head of celery, washed and chopped
4oz/125g dried chestnuts (soaked overnight and cooked until soft)
2 or 3 eating apples
$1\frac{1}{2}$ pints/850ml vegetable stock
sea salt and freshly ground black pepper
lemon juice to taste
1 tablespoon of sunflower oil
1 tablespoon of butter
some crème fraiche to serve

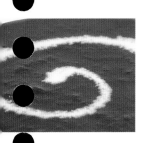

SOUP

# BRUSSELS SPROUT & CHESTNUT SOUP

Cover the chestnuts in water or stock. Cook for 10 minutes until soft, then put to one side.
Heat the oil in a large heavy-based pan and sauté the onions until they're translucent. Add the thyme and stir.
Next add the sprouts, chestnuts and their cooking liquid.
Pour in the stock and season.
Bring slowly to the boil and simmer for about 20 minutes.
Blend and season to taste.
Serve with a twirl of fresh cream.

This is one of Sarah's inventions, based on a traditional accompaniment to Christmas dinner. It's unusual, has an interesting colour, and tastes fantastic!
Plenty for four people

*i*

8oz/225g dried chestnuts (soaked overnight)
a little olive oil
2 onions, peeled and chopped
a small handful of fresh thyme
1lb 8oz/700g Brussels sprouts, peeled, trimmed and sliced
about 1 pint/600ml of very light stock
sea salt and freshly ground black pepper

# SWEET POTATO SOUP WITH CASHEW NUTS

Preheat the oven to a medium setting. In a shallow tray roast the cashew nuts until golden brown. Pour on half the tamari or soya sauce and coat the nuts evenly, then bake for a further 5 minutes until dry and crispy.

Heat the oil in a heavy-based pan; add the onion, carrots, sweet potato, chilli, ginger and garlic, and sauté until they begin to soften. Cover with stock and simmer until the vegetables are completely cooked.

Drop in the creamed coconut and the rest of the tamari or soya sauce. Allow to cool slightly. Blend. Stir in the chopped coriander.

Season to taste.

Reheat, if necessary, and serve with a few coriander leaves and a handful of warm cashew nuts sprinkled on top of each bowl.

A great cold weather soup - rich with a back-bite of chilli. This is always a big favourite in the restaurant. It seems that no matter how much we make, it always gets wiped from the blackboard - to the dismay of some waiting customers. Makes at least four big bowlfuls

*i*

8oz/225g of cashew nuts
2 tablespoon of olive oil
1 large onion, peeled and sliced
2 medium-sized carrots, peeled and sliced
1lb/450g sweet potatoes, peeled and roughly chopped
1 medium red chilli pepper, seeds removed and finely chopped
1 teaspoon of grated fresh ginger
2 cloves of garlic, peeled and crushed
$1\frac{1}{2}$ pts/850ml of vegetable stock
3oz/75g of creamed coconut
3 tablespoons of tamari or good quality soya sauce
a handful of fresh coriander, roughly chopped
(keep some leaves to garnish)
sea salt and freshly ground black pepper

19

## BASIC PASTRY CASE
## FOR SAVOURY TARTS

For a 9 inch/22cm flan tin
8oz/225g plain flour
(we use half white,
half wholemeal)
$\frac{1}{2}$ teaspoon of salt
4oz/125g butter
1 egg, beaten
(For a nutty pastry, add
$1\frac{1}{2}$oz/40g of either
roasted poppy seeds or roasted sesame seeds
to the flour)

Mix the flour and salt together. Rub
in the butter until the mixture
resembles fine breadcrumbs.
Bind with just enough cold water to make
a stiff dough. Chill for at least an hour
before using.
When required, roll out lightly and quickly
and lay on a lightly buttered flan dish.
Line the dish. Cover the pastry with baking
parchment and baking beans; bake for
20 minutes in a medium oven until the
pastry is lightly browned.
Remove the baking beans and return the
case to the oven for 5 minutes
to further cook the base.
Finally, brush the pastry with beaten egg and
put back in the oven to seal and glaze it.
(This prevents it from going soggy when the
filling is added.)

20

# SMOKED TROUT, CREAM CHEESE & DILL TART

Beat the eggs, cream and cream cheese together.
Add the chopped dill and season.
Stir in the flaked trout fillet.
Pour the mixture into the pastry case.
Place the tart in centre of a medium oven and bake until just set - about 20 minutes.
Best served warm

Serves up to eight people

*i* Basic tart pastry case - blind baked
8oz/225g smoked trout fillet, skinned and flaked
2 large eggs
$\frac{1}{2}$ pint/150ml double cream
4oz/125g full fat cream cheese
2 tablespoons of fresh chopped dill
sea salt and freshly ground black pepper

*In the mill restaurant we use local trout from the River Otter. They come from Tracey Mill at Honiton (one of the other few remaining water mills in Devon) where a number of ponds are fed by the mill race. The trout thus live in flowing water in a natural environment.*

*Wild brown trout are found in the middle and lower reaches of the river, while closer to the estuary there are visiting salmon and sea trout. And there is, reportedly, a small population of endangered white-clawed freshwater crayfish in the lower part of the river. (These are not on our menu.)*

FISH

# RICH FRUIT CAKE

Grease and line the cake tins with baking parchment.
Mix all the dry ingredients together.
Melt the margarine and add it to the mixture along with the eggs.
Beat well.
Spoon the mixture into the prepared cake tins and spread evenly.
Bake in the centre of a low oven (150°C/Gas mark 2) for about 1 to 1½ hours for smaller cakes and about 1½ to 2½ hours for a large cake.
Test to see if the cake is cooked by pressing a finger on the top and seeing if the cake springs back again, or by inserting a skewer - the skewer should come out clean.
When cooked take out of the oven and allow to cool in the tin.

You look at that and you think, 'That's Christmas done and dusted.' (John O'Hanlon)

1lb/450g wholemeal flour
1lb 10oz/725g mixed dried fruit
6oz/150g glace cherries
3oz/75g almonds
1lb/450g margarine (we use organic vegan margarine)
1lb/450g brown sugar
1 teaspoon of mixed spice
8 eggs, beaten

*This recipe has been used at Otterton Mill since the bakery first started here. Nowadays we make it with our own organic milled flour, organic ingredients and a helping of Port Stout. Lydia and Roy (see p46) call this their "off the hook" fruit cake, because it's so reliable and easy to make. It's also really versatile; just add more fruit, or more nuts, use different fruit, add different nuts, use different spices… If possible soak the dried fruit in alcohol (for at least 24 hours - a week is better). At the mill we have a large crock of steeped fruit that is constantly added to, so we always have a ready supply for the bakery! We use the wonderful O'Hanlon's Port Stout as standard (see p26-27). For Christmas and other special occasions we use Thomas Hardy Ale or one of Lyme Bay's Fruit Liqueurs such as "Apricot and Brandy" or "Whisky Ginger" (see p100-101) Leave plain or decorate extravagantly! This recipe will make two 2lb 8oz cakes (or one big 5-pounder).*

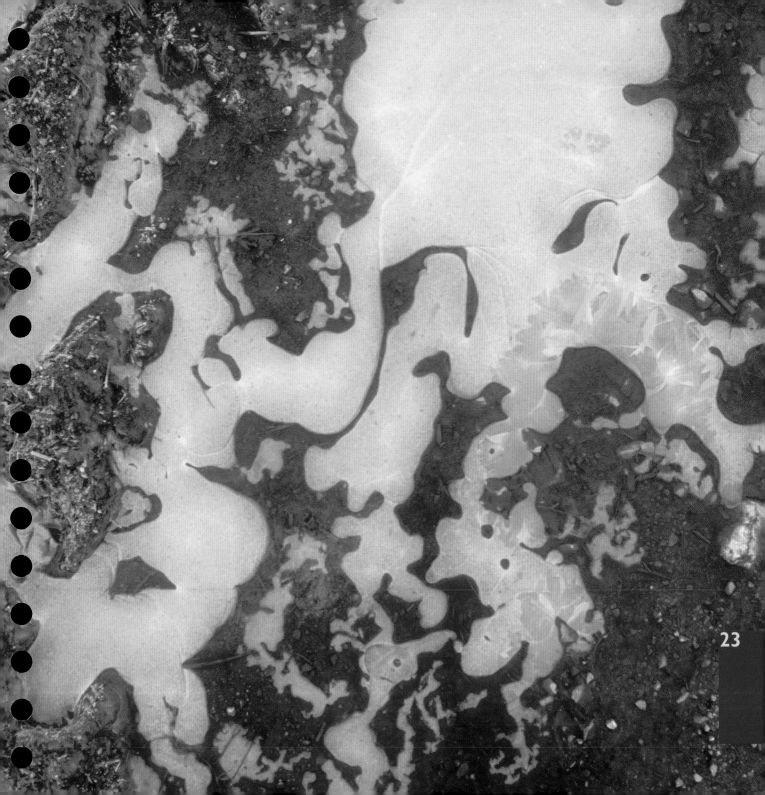

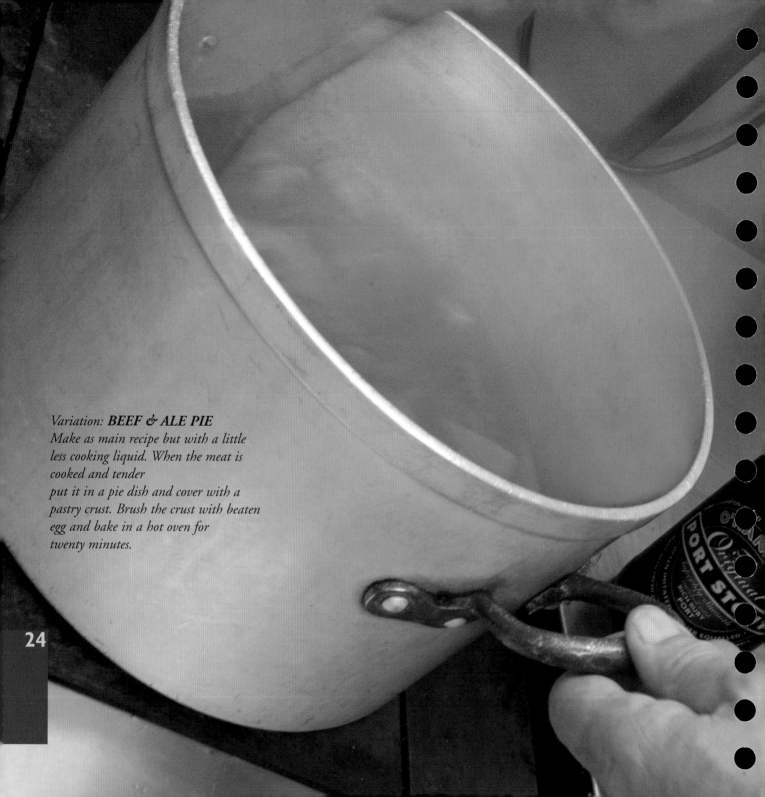

*Variation:* **BEEF & ALE PIE**
*Make as main recipe but with a little*
*less cooking liquid. When the meat is*
*cooked and tender*
*put it in a pie dish and cover with a*
*pastry crust. Brush the crust with beaten*
*egg and bake in a hot oven for*
*twenty minutes.*

24

# BEEF IN PORT STOUT

Preheat the oven to a medium setting. Heat the oil in a heavy cooking pot (one with a lid) and brown the meat well, a few pieces at a time. Put the browned meat to one side as it's done.

Add the onions, garlic, and other vegetables to the pan and soften. Sprinkle over any leftover seasoned flour and stir in.

Pour in the stout and allow to bubble for a couple of minutes.

Return the meat to the cooking pot. Then add the herbs, the orange zest, bay leaves, tomato puree and enough stock to cover it all. Put on the pot lid and simmer gently until the meat is cooked - about $1\frac{1}{2}$ hrs.

Season to taste. Possibly add a little dark brown sugar and a dash of soy sauce as well.

Good served with mashed potatoes (with some Highfield's special mustard stirred in). Or try adding diced potatoes to the cooking pot to cook along with the beef.

Six generous servings
Ian based this recipe on the traditional Flanders dish of beef carbonade. His version uses O'Hanlon's Original Port Stout for a real richness and depth of flavour.

*i*

2 tablespoon of olive oil
2 lbs/1kg of diced beef tossed in seasoned flour
2 large onions, peeled and chopped
2 to 4 garlic cloves, peeled and crushed
4 sticks of celery, chopped
2 medium-sized parsnips, peeled and sliced
2 large carrots, peeled and sliced
the zest of an orange
a large handful of fresh herbs (include thyme)
2 bay leaves, torn into pieces
$\frac{1}{2}$ litre of O'Hanlon's Original Port Stout (or similar)
a few ladlefuls of stock
1 tablespoon of tomato puree
sea salt and freshly ground black pepper

**25**

**MEAT**

## Our beer people: John and Liz O'Hanlon

*Asked if he began as a CAMRA-inspired evangelist for quality beer, John O'Hanlon looks a tiny bit apologetic and says 'No, not really. What happened was, we had our own pub in London, in Clerkenwell, and we sold a lot of what they call 'craft beers', made by smallish independent brewers. And one day I thought, Well, we could do that. So we started brewing at the back of the pub. After a while we needed more space, so we moved everything into one of those great railway arches in Vauxhall. Then, about five years ago, we decided, for all sorts of good reasons, that we needed to get the hell out of London altogether. So we brought the whole shooting-match, fermentation vessels, barrels, bottling equipment, everything, plus children and dogs and all our belongings, down here on a convoy of trucks. Fortunately, our master brewer Alex and his assistant Richard were up for it too.'*

*Which is all pretty astonishing, really, because 'here' is an ancient, higgledy-piggledy farm tucked away in one of those hidden parts of east Devon that you find only by following a narrow lane that goes from Nowhere in Particular to Nowhere in General. Then you turn off down a winding pot-holed track and just when you're thinking, No this can't be right, you arrive.*

*'We saw it for the first time on a lovely summer's day. Just as well, too, because it looked like no-one had done a thing to the house since World War Two. Or even One. Come the first winter, we had so many buckets catching leaks you could hardly move about the place. But the farm had one really important thing - a natural spring that gave us good pure water. We started brewing within four weeks of getting here.'*

*There's no secret to good brewing, according to John. 'You just start with the very best ingredients you can find. Then you do incredibly careful and complicated things with them. And you have to be prepared for the fact that you'll make mistakes, especially when you're developing a new beer.' He nods towards a drain in the brewhouse floor. 'We've had to pour thousands of litres of mistakes down there.'*

*The O'Hanlons get it right, though. Their beers and ales have won more medals than you'd normally find on a Latin American dictator's chest. As well as producing their own beers, they've turned to resurrecting 'lost classics' such as Royal Oak, which vanished from the market when its brewer was swallowed up by some galloping monopoly. Within months of the O'Hanlon Brewery reproducing it to its original 1896 recipe it won the Gold at the Brewing Industry International Awards. (And quickly became a firm favourite here at the Mill.) More recently, they've revived Thomas Hardy's Ale, first brewed half a century ago. 'When we got hold of what they called the recipe it looked hopeless. A single sheet of A4 which gave us more or less nothing apart from the raw ingredients. Eventually we discovered that the master brewer who'd first made it was still alive and persuaded him to come down here and help us reconstruct the process. It was a slow and complex business, but we're pretty pleased with it.' Indeed. It's an amazing drink. Very strong (11.7% ABV), rich, velvety, packed with malt, hop, and chocolatey flavours, it's more like a liqueur than an ale. It comes in small limited-edition bottles which are much in demand in countries as diverse as Chile and Japan. And, according to John, it improves with age; a bottle bought now might well peak in twenty years' time. (If you've a little less patience, it will put power into your next Christmas cake - see p22.)*

(see p22.)

Combine the ingredients for the marinade using either a food processor or a mortar and pestle. Add sufficient olive oil to make a loose paste.

Rub the marinade all over the pork, working it into the scoring in the rind and where the bone has been removed. Pour the orange wine over the pork and leave to marinate overnight, or for as long as possible, in the fridge.

Roll the meat up and tie it with string. Place the joint on the bones, with the sliced onion underneath, in a large roasting pan.

Pour over any remaining marinade. Sprinkle the pork rind well with sea salt.

Put in a pre-heated hot oven and cook for about 1 hour before adding the diced sweet potatoes. Use the meat fat to baste the sweet potatoes.

Bake for a further 40 minutes or until the meat is well cooked, the crackling crisp and the potatoes soft.

Rest the meat and potatoes in a warm place for at least 15 minutes. Make a simple sauce by draining any fat from the roasting pan and stirring a little more orange wine into the onions and juices that are left. Allow to bubble over a fairly low heat. Season to taste.

Pour the sauce over some chunky slices of pork and a few sweet potatoes.

Serve and enjoy!

MARINADE
4 tablespoons fennel seeds, roasted and crushed
3 star anise
1 teaspoon of dill seeds
sea salt and freshly ground black pepper
3 bay leaves
a large handful of fresh chopped dill
the zest of a couple of oranges
some olive oil

# ROAST LOIN OF PORK WITH A SPICED ORANGE RUB & ROASTED SWEET POTATOES

This makes enough to serve six to eight people

*i* 5 lb/2½ kilo leg of pork de-boned. Leave the skin on and make sure that it is well scored through to encourage crackling. (Keep the bones to use as a roasting rack and to improve the sauce)
1 onion, peeled and sliced
2 tablespoons of Lyme Bay Orange Wine (see p100-101)
sea salt
1 sweet potato per person chopped in large chunks, skin left on

*Devon is home to some of the country's leading free-range pork producers - we get ours from Kenniford Farm near the Mill.*
*Jill got the idea for this recipe from an old, well-thumbed, Tamsin Day-Lewis cookery book.*

MEAT

Pre-heat oven to a hot setting. Scrub and chop the root vegetables into bite-sized pieces. (Cut any swede a bit smaller as it takes a little longer to cook).

Put the onions and garlic into a large shallow ovenproof dish. Scatter the chopped vegetables on top and liberally drizzle olive oil over them. Sprinkle with thyme and lots of seasoning.

Roast in a hot oven until the vegetables are cooked. About 45 minutes.

Make a roux by stirring the flour into the oil and melted butter over a medium heat. Add the wine gradually, stirring continually to avoid lumps. Add the stock and stir. Finally, add the cream, season to taste and cook gently.

Mix the topping ingredients together to make a crumble. Pour the sauce over the vegetables. Sprinkle the crumble on top.

Bake in a medium hot oven for 15 to 20 minutes until golden brown and bubbling.

# ROASTED ROOT CRUNCH PIE

Makes enough for four to six.

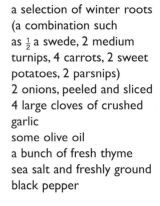

a selection of winter roots
(a combination such
as $\frac{1}{2}$ a swede, 2 medium
turnips, 4 carrots, 2 sweet
potatoes, 2 parsnips)
2 onions, peeled and sliced
4 large cloves of crushed
garlic
some olive oil
a bunch of fresh thyme
sea salt and freshly ground
black pepper

FOR THE SAUCE
1oz/25g butter
1 tablespoon of olive oil
2 tablespoons of plain flour
about 5fl oz/150ml white
wine
about 5fl oz/150ml
vegetable stock
8 fl oz/250ml double cream
seasoning

FOR THE TOPPING
6oz/175g fresh
breadcrumbs
3oz/75g mixed toasted
seeds
2oz/50g toasted oats
2oz/50g grated cheese
1oz/25g melted butter

*In the chilly grey days of winter the sweet earthy flavours of root vegetables are very comforting.*

Put the cubes of aubergine in a sieve and sprinkle them with salt. Leave for 10 minutes or so to draw out the bitterness, then rinse and dry.

Heat the oil in a heavy-based pan (one with a lid) and sauté the onion and garlic for a few minutes. Add the aubergine and the mushrooms and soften them.

Stir in the tomatoes and wine and cook until bubbling.

Cover the pan, lower the heat and let it simmer until the vegetables are soft.

Stir in the basil and the cashew nuts or walnuts.

Season to taste. The flavour should be intense and dark!

To make the risotto heat the olive oil in a heavy-based frying pan (one with a lid) add the buckwheat and let it fry in the oil for a few minutes until it is hot and starting to brown slightly. Then add the onion and lightly sauté it.

Pour in the hot stock so that the contents of the pan are just covered and leave over a low heat with the lid on the pan until the liquid is absorbed. The grains should be fluffy but still separate and slightly firm. This will take about 5 minutes.

Season if necessary.

Serve a large spoonful of the aubergine ragout over the buckwheat with a good dollop of sour cream on top and a basil leaf to garnish.

# AUBERGINE RAGOUT WITH BUCKWHEAT RISOTTO

Enough to serve four

1 large aubergine, cut in half lengthways and cubed.
2 tablespoons of olive oil
8oz/225g mushrooms washed and halved, or quartered, depending on size
1 large onion, chopped
2 to 4 cloves of crushed garlic
a large handful of fresh basil, chopped or torn
400g tin of chopped tomatoes
$\frac{1}{2}$ glass of red wine
2oz/50g roasted cashew nuts, or walnuts
sea salt and freshly ground black pepper
2 tablespoons of olive oil
1 large onion, chopped
8oz/225g buckwheat
1 pint/600ml of hot vegetable stock
a carton of sour cream

31

VEG

# LAMB TAGINE WITH CHICKPEAS, CINNAMON & APRICOTS

This is one of our musician chef Ian's recipes. When Ian was recording his album Blues Avenue in Bristol, he ate daily at a small Moroccan street restaurant and loved their lamb tagine so much it inspired him to create his own version.

Enough to serve four

1 or 2 tablespoons olive oil
1lb 8oz/700g stewing lamb (shoulder or neck) cut into medium-sized chunks
1 onion - peeled and chopped
2 cloves garlic - peeled and crushed
a stick of cinnamon
1 tablespoon of ground cumin
1 tablespoon of ground coriander
1 heaped teaspoon of turmeric
$\frac{1}{2}$ teaspoon ground cloves
a can of chopped tomatoes
$\frac{1}{2}$ pint/300ml of stock
sea salt and freshly ground black pepper
8oz/225g cooked chickpeas, drained
3oz/75g dried apricots, roughly chopped
1 tablespoon of runny honey
8oz/225g couscous
$\frac{1}{2}$ pint/300ml hot vegetable stock (use the liquid from the chickpeas)
a large handful of fresh coriander - finely chopped

Heat the oil in a large flameproof casserole and brown the lamb in batches. Remove from the pan and put to one side when done.
Fry the onion for about 5 minutes, until soft. Add the garlic, cinnamon, cumin, coriander, turmeric and cloves and fry another minute or so.
Add the tomatoes and the stock and bring to the boil. Then return the lamb to the casserole. Season, cover and simmer.
After an hour, add the chickpeas, prunes and the honey. Continue to simmer gently for another 30 minutes until the meat is really tender.
Add a little water if the liquid has reduced - make sure there is plenty of rich sauce.
Before serving, pour the hot stock over the couscous and leave it to be absorbed. Fluff up with a fork, season with salt and pepper and stir in the chopped coriander.
Ladle the tagine over the couscous.

33

MEAT

# CHESTNUT, MUSHROOM, CRANBERRY & SPINACH FILO PARCELS

Cook the cranberries in a pan with sufficient water to just cover them. When soft, sweeten with a little brown sugar and check their sharpness - they should be tart. Allow to cool.

Cook the chestnuts in water until soft enough to break into pieces but not soft enough to puree. Drain and cool.

Heat the olive oil in a pan and sauté the garlic and onion until softened. Add the mushrooms and cook for a further 2 to 3 minutes. Pour in the red wine, heat until bubbling, and season.

Mix the cornflour with just enough water to dissolve it. Add to the pan, stirring as it thickens. Take off the heat and add the drained cranberries, chestnuts and spinach. It should be a fairly stiff mixture.

This recipe was created when Ian ran his own restaurant in Taunton. It was intended to be a vegetarian Christmas dish, but it stayed on the menu and became known as 'Popeye's Build Up' because of the spinach and hearty content. Enough to make about six to eight parcels

Set the oven to a medium setting. Unfold the filo pastry sheets, take one sheet and lay it out. Cut in half to form two squares. Brush one square with melted butter or oil. Place the second square on top of the first square and at 45° to it, and brush with oil.

Spoon a generous tablespoon of the mixture into the centre of the filo. Pull the edges up together over the filling, and squeeze and twist together to form a small parcel. Brush the top with butter or oil.

Place the parcels on a greased baking tray and bake in the oven for 20 to 25 min until lightly browned and bubbling.

*i* 4oz/125g cranberries
a little brown sugar
8oz/225g dried chestnuts, soaked overnight
2 tablespoons of olive oil
1 clove of crushed garlic
1 medium onion, finely chopped
8oz/225g mushrooms, sliced
$\frac{1}{2}$ glass red wine
sea salt and freshly ground black pepper
1 tablespoon of cornflour
8oz/225g spinach, cooked and chopped
1 packet of filo pastry. melted butter or olive oil for brushing

34

VEG

### Our cheese people: Gary and Elise of Country Cheeses, Tavistock

*As with many enthusiastic food specialists, it was frustration, rather than 'spotting a gap in the market', that got Gary and Elise going, fifteen years ago.*

*'We live in Sampford Courtney and just up the road, at Jacobstowe, there was a cheesemaker called Rachel Stevens who was making fabulous stuff. But hardly anyone sold it. Shops sold mass-produced rubbery cheddar and imported French cheeses. But great quality locally-produced cheese? Forget it. We're vegetarians, and cheese was and is an important part of our diet. And we thought that it was all wrong that there were great cheeses out there, but most people had no opportunity to buy them.'*

*So Elise and Gary's mum set up shop in Tavistock's beautiful old Pannier Market.*

*'We started with a table with just a few different cheeses on it: Rachel's, some of Quicke's cheddar from Newton St Cyres, and one or two others. It was really, really slow at first. But then it started to snowball.'*

*Indeed it did, because if you go into either of their shops now you'll find scores and scores of lovingly-crafted cheeses, of an amazing variety of textures, aromas, flavours, and shapes. The names are wonderful: Tiskey Meadow, Somerset Rambler, Vulscombe, Little Stinky, Beenleigh Blue, Menallack, Sharpham's Rustic, Ticklemore, Withybrook Pyramid… Where did they all come from? Have they always existed, secretly? 'Yes and no,' Gary says. 'Until about the middle of the last century, lots of diary farmers - or their wives, probably - made their own unique cheeses. But cheesemaking is a slow, patient and tricky business, so when the Milk Marketing Board and mass-production came along, a lot of them gave up what they saw as another chore. So when we started, we had to go cheese-hunting, tracking down people who were still working in that old-fashioned small-scale way. But in recent years there's been a huge revival. Part of it is down to the fact that farmers have been put under economic pressure to diversify, then there's been this recent upsurge of interest in quality food, of people caring about what they eat.'*

*Gary doesn't say so, but he and Elise are themselves another reason for the Great Cheese Renaissance, because it would come to nothing without committed and expert retailers. And they commission their own cheeses, too. Bakesey Meadow and Chemmy are differently delicious goats' milk cheeses, and Celeste is a rich, Camembert-style cheese made from Jersey cows' milk; all three are made exclusively for them by Debbie Mumford of the Sharpham Estate.*

*In both their shops customers are encouraged to have a little taste before they buy, because, as with wine, all sorts of things - the weather, what animals graze on, tiny variations in the maturing conditions - can cause subtle variations in flavour.*

*'If a cheese is exactly the same all the time, you might want to ask yourself why,' Gary says, darkly. 'In our shop, though, all our cheeses are consistently wonderful rather than wonderfully consistent.' Which, you might think, is a cheesey line; but it's true.*

36

MILLER'S LUNCH - local Devon cheese, chutney,
fresh crusty bread and a plate of salads. Excellent
with a glass of cider (see p100).

## The Rhyming Miller and the Law

*In the mid 19th century, the miller was a fellow called John Uglow who, at great expense, imported two sets of French millstones. He was, naturally, very proud of these stones and had them carved with commemorative rhymes:*

*This stone worked the first time, March 28th, 1859*
*This stone worked the first time, tis true, May 1st, 1862.*

*One hopes that his flour was less lumpy than his verse. Uglow's millstones are still here; they're on view upstairs in the gallery.*

*It's hard to believe, perhaps, but Otterton was a bit on the rough side back in John Uglow's day. There was a good deal of poaching and smuggling and general skulduggery in and around the place. So the miller took it upon himself to introduce constables to the village, arming them with pistols and cutlasses. This did not go down at all well with the lawless Ottertonians, who made their feelings known by shinning over the mill walls and cutting down all of Uglow's fruit trees.*

*He retaliated by getting himself a ground patrol of bull mastiffs who sported huge spiked brass collars with 'Otterton Mills' engraved upon them. Relations between village and mill have improved since then, although our cockerels can sometimes be slightly territorial…*

# BEETROOT, ORANGE & PARSLEY SALAD

Put the grated beetroot into a large
bowl. Add enough olive oil to coat
the beetroot and stir.
Add the lemon juice, orange zest
and juice, and the orange segments
and mix well.
Add the chopped parsley and season.

2 large raw beetroot, peeled and grated
olive oil
juice of a lemon
zest and juice of an orange
2 oranges, peeled and segmented
a large bunch of fresh parsley, finely chopped
sea salt and freshly ground black pepper

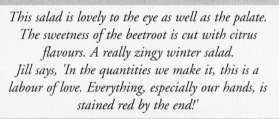

*This salad is lovely to the eye as well as the palate.*
*The sweetness of the beetroot is cut with citrus*
*flavours. A really zingy winter salad.*
*Jill says, 'In the quantities we make it, this is a*
*labour of love. Everything, especially our hands, is*
*stained red by the end!'*

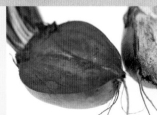

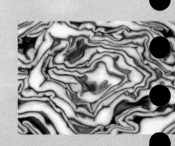

## RED CABBAGE, APPLE & CINNAMON SALAD

## CELERIAC, CARROT & FENNEL SEED SALAD

Combine the sliced cabbage and the apples, toss and mix in the lemon juice then add the oil.  Sprinkle in the cinnamon and add the apple juice and mix well.
Season to taste.
Leave to stand for a short while.
Mix again before serving.

Mix the celeriac and carrots. Add the lemon juice and stir in. Add the rest of the ingredients and mix well.

half a red cabbage, very finely sliced and chopped into about 2 inch/5 cm lengths
3 cox's apples, washed but unpeeled, quartered, cored and sliced finely
the juice of a lemon
1 tablespoon of sunflower oil
1 teaspoon of fresh ground cinnamon
2 or 3 tablespoons of apple juice concentrate (or use fresh and add a dash of honey too)
sea salt and freshly ground black pepper

one medium-sized celeriac, peeled and coarsely grated
the same weight in carrots, peeled and coarsely grated
juice of a lemon
zest of an orange
2 tablespoons of fennel seeds, toasted
2 tablespoons of sunflower oil
1 tablespoon of runny honey
sea salt and freshly ground black pepper

*This salad has wonderful crispness and colour. When the cinnamon is first added it makes the salad very brown; but let it stand for about 15 minutes and the redness of the cabbage really comes through.*

SALAD

# LEMON TART

Pre-heat the oven to medium-low.
Put the eggs and the sugar into a
deep bowl and mix until blended.
(Don't beat too hard; try to avoid a
lot of frothing).
Stir in the lemon zest and juice.
Gently stir in the cream and pour the
mixture slowly into the pastry case.
Bake for 30 to 35 minutes until the
tart has just set but still wobbles.
Remove from oven and allow to cool.
Serve dusted with icing.

According to Sarah, this is
the culinary equivalent of
the Little Black Dress:
indispensable,
reliable, and suitable
for any occasion.

a 9 inch/22cm sweet
pastry case
4 eggs
8oz/225g light soft brown
sugar
the zest and juice of 3 to
5 unwaxed organic
lemons - very finely
grated. (If you don't want
'bits' in the tart, add the
zest to the juice and
strain before use.)
6 fl oz/180ml double
cream
icing sugar for dusting

*SWEET PASTRY*
*FOR OPEN TARTS*
*For a 9 inch/22cm flan tin*
*9oz/250g flour*
*3oz/75g vanilla caster sugar*
*6oz/175g butter*

*Mix the flour and sugar together in
a bowl.*
*Melt the butter and mix into the
flour and sugar to make a paste.
Then press the mix into the flan
tin rather than roll it.
Bake in a medium oven for 15 to 20
minutes until light golden brown.
(Add the zest of a lemon to the dry
flour/sugar mix for a lemon pastry;
orange zest for orange pastry
and so on.)*

# CHOCOLATE & CHESTNUT MARQUISE

Grease and line a loaf tin with baking parchment.

Put the chestnuts into a food processor with the melted butter and all but 1 tablespoon of the sugar. Blend.

Melt the chocolate with the brandy and the water in a heatproof bowl over a pan of simmering water, stirring until smooth. (Or use a microwave). Add to the chestnut mixture and blend again.

Add the egg yolks, one at a time.

In a large bowl whisk the egg whites to soft peaks and then add the remaining tablespoon of sugar. Whisk again until stiff.

Stir a spoonful of the chestnut-chocolate mixture into the egg whites and then fold the rest in. The mixture will be sort of stiff and sludgy.

Pour the mixture into the prepared loaf tin and then leave to chill in the fridge.

Turn out onto a flat plate and serve in slices with pouring cream. (You could add an extra dash of brandy to the cream if you're feeling wicked.)

Even if you are not a big fan of chestnuts they do combine wonderfully with chocolate to make this simple dessert that shouts 'winter is here, time to wrap up and indulge'.

7oz/200g chestnuts, cooked
4oz/125g melted butter
4oz/125g vanilla sugar
7oz/200g dark chocolate (70% cocoa solids), broken into pieces
1 tablespoon of apple brandy
1 tablespoon of water
4 eggs, separated

SWEET

# WARM POLENTA CAKE WITH SPICED PLUMS

Grease an 8 inch/20cm
cake tin and line the base with
baking parchment.
Set the oven to medium-low.

Beat the butter and sugar together
until light and fluffy.
Whizz or chop the blanched almonds
into small pieces (not too fine).
Add the chopped and the ground
almonds to the butter and sugar
mixture and stir in.
Break the eggs into a small bowl and
beat them lightly with a fork. Stir into
the mixture.
Then gently stir in the polenta, baking
powder, orange zest, juice and
crushed cardamom seeds.
Pour the mixture into the prepared
cake tin and level the surface.
Bake for 30 minutes. Turn the oven
down a little and bake for a further
20 to 30 minutes, or until the cake is
firm to the touch.

While the cake is baking, make a
syrup by putting the lemon and
orange juice and the honey into a
small stainless steel saucepan. Bring
to the boil and stir for a few minutes.
While the cake is still warm, make a
few holes in the top, with a skewer,
and spoon the warm syrup over.
Leave to cool.

Finally, prepare the spiced plums.
Put the apple juice in a small pan
with the spices and bring to the boil.
Add the plums and simmer for about
10 minutes until cooked. Sweeten
with a little honey or sugar to taste.
Allow to cool slightly before serving
a tablespoon of the spiced plums
with a portion of cake.

42

SWEET

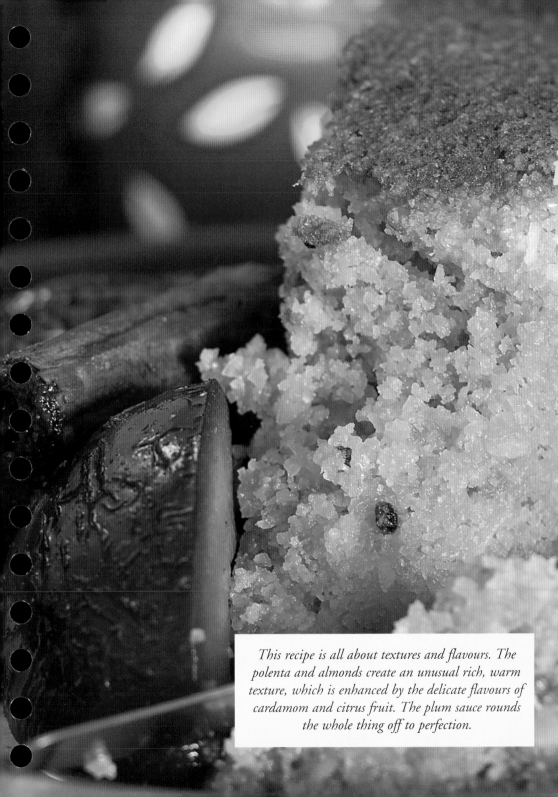

8oz/225g butter, softened
8oz/225g soft light
brown sugar
5oz/150g blanched
almonds
5oz/150g ground
almonds
3 large eggs
5oz/150g polenta
1 teaspoon of baking
powder
the zest of an orange,
finely grated
the juice of an orange
12 green cardamom
seeds, crushed

SYRUP
the juice of 2 lemons
the juice of 2 oranges
4 tablespoons of honey

SPICED PLUMS
2 or 3 tablespoon of
apple juice or water
$\frac{1}{2}$ stick of cinnamon
3 cloves
1 teaspoon of mixed
spice
1 star anise
8 sharp plums, stoned
and halved
a little honey or brown
sugar to taste

*This recipe is all about textures and flavours. The
polenta and almonds create an unusual rich, warm
texture, which is enhanced by the delicate flavours of
cardamom and citrus fruit. The plum sauce rounds
the whole thing off to perfection.*

SWEET

BIRDS SINGING

FIRST SPRING FLOWERS – DAFFODILS, CROCUS & SNOWDROPS

SENSE OF ANTICIPATION

EASTER AND THREE BUSY BANK HOLIDAYS

PLANTING

MUSIC EVENINGS BEGIN

WISTERIA IN BLOOM

CHICKENS LAYING

CHESTNUT FLOWERING

EELS RETURN TO THE LEAT

44

SPRING

## Otterton Mill Bakery

*All the bread made in the Mill Bakery is made by hand. This gives our bakers far more control over the process; it also makes it hard and muscular work. We produce several hundred loaves a day.*

*So it helps that Roy Hamilton is a smiling tower of a man.*

*Roy is passionate about the whole unpredictable nature of the baking process. As he examines a loaf of walnut bread, fresh out of the oven and smelling unbelievably good, he says that baking is all about feeling and intuition.*

*'It's the first time I've made this bread,' he says.*

*'I chickened out a bit, though; it should have had another 20 minutes to rise.'*

*When he was pretty young, Roy went skiing in Germany and discovered the local 'real' bread. He got himself a job as a waiter, saw the bread being made and that was it; he was hooked. Back in England he went off to college, intending to study engineering. By one of those fortunate mishaps, the course was oversubscribed, so he signed up for bakery instead. Since then he has worked for large and small supermarkets, for a Jewish bakery that specialised in big rye loaves, and in New Zealand, where he baked in the mornings and managed a YHA hostel in the evenings.*

*But Roy's big learning experience was at the Village Bakery in Cumbria where he worked with Paul Merry, maestro of the traditional wood-fired masonry oven. At The Village Bakery the ovens are rigged with a simple conveyor system that drops loaves, via flap doors, directly onto the oven bottom. 'There's nothing like a hot oven bottom... ... you get that wonderful caramelised crust,' Roy says; he's planning to get wood-fired bread ovens built at the Mill. In the meantime, he continues joyously to experiment and perfect. 'It's just a knead I have,' he claims. (He's better at buns than puns.)*

*Lydia Greenaway always knew she wanted to cook. After college, one of her first jobs was cooking cordon bleu food in Hampshire for the directors of John Lewis. Since then, she's cooked in several places throughout Devon, and had her own restaurant in Budleigh Salterton. She was recruited from the village bakery soon after the Mill was renovated, about 12 years ago. She still bakes some bread but, as a not very large person, was glad to hand the bulk of that very physical job over to Roy.*

*Now Lydia is our cake-maker. She often makes about 120 cakes a day, plus trays of flapjack and fruit slices, and several batches of scones. Cakes may not be quite such hard work to make as bread but they're still all handmade. In the quantities that Lydia uses rubbing butter into flour is a daunting task.*

47

# BLACK OLIVE & CORIANDER BREAD

Mix the yeast and sugar together in a cup of the warm water until smooth. Stir all the dough ingredients together (except the rest of the warm water) in a large bowl. Add the yeast mixture and work into the dough with your hands. Add more of the water if needed to form a uniform soft ball. Cover the bowl and leave to rise for about 30 minutes.

Put the onions, coriander and olives into a food processor and chop them coarsely.

Remove the dough from the bowl and knead it for 5 minutes, return to the bowl and leave until recovered.

Turn the dough out onto a floured surface. Roll it into a rectangle about 8 inches/20cm by 10 inches/25cm. Take care that the dough does not stick to the table.

Cover the rectangle of dough with the olive filling as evenly as possible. Then roll the shorter edge over onto the surface of the filling and continue to roll it all up like a swiss roll.

Place the rolled dough, seam side down, into an oiled medium to large bread tin.

Push a few pitted olives into top of the bread.

Allow the bread to rise in a warm place (the airing cupboard is good if you don't mind a lingering whiff of onion and olive).

Bake at 220°C/Gas mark 7 for about 20 minutes - light bake

While the bread is still in the tin brush the top with olive oil and then immediately take it out and put the loaf onto a cooling rack. Do this quickly because otherwise the loaf may stick.

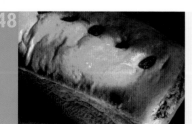

48

*Excellent with good local cheese (see p35) and wine or one of our fine local beers (see p26-27) but if there's a bread that can stand on its own - eaten straight from the oven - then this is it. Always make more than you think you'll eat!*

**DOUGH**
1lb/450g unbleached white flour
2oz/50g whole-wheat flour
2oz/50g fresh yeast
1oz/25g dark brown sugar
2 tablespoons of olive oil
the brine from a tin of olives (see below)
1 dessert spoon of ground coriander
about $\frac{1}{2}$ pint/300ml of warm water (30°C)

**FILLING**
1 large onion
2oz/50g fresh coriander
1 x 400g tin of pitted black olives in brine
- put a few to one side for decoration

# ORANGE & POPPY SEED CAKE

Grease and line an 8 inch/20cm cake tin.
Cream the margarine and sugar together in a bowl until pale and fluffy. Add all the other ingredients and beat well.
Spoon the mixture into the prepared tin and bake for 40 minutes at 170°C/Gas mark 3 until lightly golden brown and firm to touch.
Turn out of the tin and cool

This is a really quick and easy cake to make. It also makes a great pudding - serve warm with an orange sauce and some thick Devon cream.

*i* 6oz/175g margarine
6oz/175g caster sugar
8oz/225g unbleached white flour
1 teaspoon of baking powder
3 eggs
the zest of an orange
2oz/50g poppy seeds

50

SWEET

### Our organic wheat people: Tamarisk Farm

*We all know that there's nothing idyllic about farming, these days. Dirty work, long hours, tight margins, hard choices. Survive by selling off a couple of acres for 'executive housing', maybe; do B&B, have holiday caravans in a field, hustle diminishing subsidies. Try to flog veg from a stall at the farm gate in the rain. No sane person would do it. All the same, standing with Ellen Simon while she summons her herd of Devon Ruby Red cattle (she does it by yelling 'Caa-ttle! Caa-ttle!' like Joyce Grenfell in wellies, and they do come) you could just think 'Well, yes, this is the life.' Because this part of Tamarisk Farm is, officially as well as actually, beautiful. It's an area of Outstanding Natural Beauty, part of the Dorset Heritage Coast, and there's a Site of Special Scientific Interest slap in the middle of it. It overlooks a great sweep of Lyme Bay. The fields, separated by hedges and patches of gorse and thorn frosted with wild clematis, slope down to the sea. Chesil Beach arcs eastwards towards Portland Bill, humped on the silver horizon. Larks improvise. A kestrel lifts off from a wind-tilted copse.*

*Forty years ago, some chaps from the government gazed at this view and decided that it would be a good spot to build a nuclear power station. This rather upset Ellen's parents.*

*Arthur and Josephine Pearse became farmers 'by accident' (according to Arthur, who is very partial to understatement). They bought Manor Cottage in 1945, put their stuff in it, then went off to teach in Nigeria. When they returned to West Bexington they started small-scale market gardening. They bought the farmyard and its dilapidated buildings opposite the cottage, and an extra acre of land for their vegetables. By the mid-sixties, the Pearses had 'sort of accidentally', acquired several more acres and the market garden had evolved into a farm.*

*They were 'organic' before anyone used the term. Arthur denies that there was anything ideological about it. He claims that he just wasn't clever enough to use chemicals. (Adam Simon, Ellen's husband, laughs at this.) He says Josephine merely thought that 'it would be better for the children'. In fact, they had witnessed agrochemical disasters in West Africa, and were among the earliest members of the Soil Association.*

*When the Men from the Ministry showed up some of the locals responded to the nuclear threat by covenanting their land to the National Trust. This, according to Ellen, was a pivotal moment. Since then, the NT has acquired over 700 miles of coastline and some 55,000 hectares of coastal hinterland important for its historic or landscape value. Gradually - encouraged and pressurized by people like the Tamarisk clan - the Trust began to evolve from minders of stately homes and gardens into an organically-oriented conservationist organisation. This at a time when farmers were being subsidised to level copses and grub up hedgerows that stood in the way of mechanisation; when only 'cranks' used words like 'habitat' and 'ecology' in the same sentence as 'agriculture'.*

*Now, in partnership with the Trust, the Pearses and Simons manage 600 acres, including the beautiful (if discouragingly named) Labour in Vain farm, which neighbours Tamarisk to the east, and Cogden, the permanent pasture where the Ruby Reds and the black Hebridean sheep graze. As well as the wheat we mill at Otterton, Tamarisk produces organic rye, beef, mutton and lamb. And, of course, vegetables. Spending a morning with Ellen and her family is an intensive - if somewhat bewildering - educational experience. Conversation switches between the nesting requirements of stone-chats and the price of diesel, the politics of conservation and the relative hoof-sizes of different cattle breeds, EU subsidies and local geology, fast food and foot-and-mouth, dry stone walling and bread recipes, buzzards and thatching reed. It all makes sense if you know how it fits together.*

# PAN GALLEGOS BREAD

Mix the yeast and the sugar with a little warm water.

Put the flours, salt and millet in a large bowl.

When the yeast starts to foam add it to the dry ingredients in the bowl.

Add the rest of the warm water and stir to form a smooth dough. Knead until smooth and even in consistency. Cover and leave until the dough doubles in size - about 20 minutes.

Remove the dough from bowl, add the seeds and knead for a further 5 minutes, return to bowl for another 10 minutes.

Shape into a round and then pat all over with olive oil. Put a little polenta into the bowl and drop the dough in, turn the dough around in the bowl until it is covered with the polenta.

Put onto a large baking tray that has been dusted with polenta

Dust the top with extra polenta and then using your fingertips pinch the centre section of the loaf to create small indentions, as a pattern, on top of the bread

Bake at 240°C/Gas mark 9 for approx 35 to 40 minutes (light bake).

The bottom of the loaf should sound hollow when tapped. Put onto a wire rack to cool.

This is a traditional Spanish bread from Galicia.

*i*

1oz/25g fresh yeast
$\frac{1}{2}$ teaspoon dark brown sugar
14oz/400g unbleached white flour
4oz/125g whole-wheat flour
$\frac{1}{2}$ teaspoon salt
1oz/25g millet
1oz/25g pumpkin seeds
1oz/25g sunflower seeds
$\frac{1}{2}$ pint/300 ml of lukewarm water
1 tablespoon olive oil
some dry polenta for dusting

BAKERY

# SPICY CREAMED SPINACH & COCONUT SOUP

Serves four to six

Heat the oil in a heavy-based pan (one with a lid) and add the onion, garlic and ground cumin. Stir and cook for a few minutes until softened. Add the potato, cover the pan with a lid, and sweat over a very gentle heat for 10 minutes - without browning the vegetables.

Add the vegetable stock, bring to the boil and simmer for a further 10 minutes.

Drop in the creamed coconut and stir. Stir in the finely chopped spinach and allow to cook gently for a few minutes - so as not to loose the spinach's intense green colour. Blend until smooth.

Season and serve with a swirl of yoghurt or sour cream and some fresh coriander leaves sprinkled on top.

*i*

2 tablespoons of olive oil
2 onions, peeled and diced
2 cloves of crushed garlic
1 tablespoon of freshly ground cumin
1 potato, peeled or scrubbed, and diced
2 pints/1 litre of vegetable stock
3oz/75g creamed coconut
sea salt, lots of freshly ground black pepper and lemon juice to season
2 lbs/1 kilo spinach, washed and chopped finely
fresh coriander and some sour cream or yoghurt to serve

Heat the oil and a little butter in a heavy-based pan (one with a lid) and soften the onions, garlic and potato. Add the mushrooms, stir, put the lid on the pan and leave them to soften for a few minutes.

Pour in the warm stock and simmer gently until the potatoes and mushrooms are cooked. Then add the watercress and cook for a few minutes more, the flavour and colour of the soup is better if this is lightly cooked.

Blend. You may want to adjust the consistency of the soup by adding a little cream or milk.

Season to taste. A dash of soy sauce helps to bring out the mushroom flavour. Serve with a swirl of cream.

### GARLIC AND HERB CROUTONS

*Take a day-old Otterton Mill loaf of bread (use focaccia if you can), remove the crusts and cut into large cubes. Lightly oil a deep baking tray and throw the cubes of bread in. Sprinkle them with some good dried Provencal herbs and season with salt and black pepper. Add as many crushed cloves of garlic as you wish and drizzle with good olive oil.*

*Mix well and put into in a hot oven for about 15 minutes, or until crisp, light golden brown and smelling delicious! Sprinkle generously on soups.*

*They will keep in an airtight container for a few days.*

# WATERCRESS & MUSHROOM SOUP

Enough for four

1 tablespoon of sunflower oil
a little butter
2 large onions, peeled and chopped
2 to 4 cloves of crushed garlic
1 large potato, peeled and chopped
1 lb/450g of mushrooms, washed and roughly chopped
2 or 3 bunches of watercress, washed and chopped (use the stalks too)
2 pints/1 litre of warm vegetable stock
sea salt and freshly ground black pepper
a dash of soy sauce
a little cream or milk

*Spring is the time to switch from thick and hearty winter soups to lighter, more delicate ones. The soups in this section are perfect for bright, crisp, blustery spring days, or early summer evenings.*

SOUP

# CARROT, PARSNIP & PEANUT SOUP

Heat the oil in a large heavy-based pan. Add all the vegetables. Stir and leave over a gentle heat for 10 minutes until they have softened. Pour in the warm vegetable stock and add the peanut butter. Cook until the vegetables are soft.
Allow to cool a little. Blend.
Season to taste.

Serve with coriander leaves on top to garnish. Or add a dollop of crème fraiche and make a star shape by laying some cut pieces of chive on top.

Serves four

2 tablespoons of sunflower oil
2 medium onions, peeled and chopped
3 large carrots, peeled and chopped
3 large parsnips, peeled and chopped
2 to 4 cloves of garlic, peeled and crushed
1 heaped tablespoon of peanut butter - crunchy or smooth
2 pints/1 litre of warm vegetable stock
sea salt and freshly ground black pepper

57

SOUP

It's hard to imagine now, but until about four hundred years ago Otterton was one of the busiest ports on the south Devon coast. The Otter's estuary was much bigger and deeper back then, and Otterton was easily reached by boat; the village also had one of the largest fishing fleets in the county.
Writing in 1532, John Leyland makes it sound charming:

Otterton, a pretty fisher town,
standeth on the east side of the haven.
About a mile from Ottermouth,
and on the west side is Budleigh.

But during the latter part of the 16th century a shingle bar developed at the river mouth and the river gradually silted up. Ships could no longer reach Otterton. Its fishing boats had to move down to the mouth of the estuary, to Budleigh, and Otterton's glory days as a hub of trade drew to a close.

Budleigh was a salter town. Salt production was by means of evaporating seawater in shallow beds. For a long time, the business - and it was a good business, salt being then the main means of preserving meat and fish - was dominated by the monks of Otterton Priory. (Monks were usually the keenest of entrepreneurs, until Henry VIII put the dampers on things.) The Otterton brothers brought salt up from Budleigh and dried it in salt pans over open fires, then traded it up the Otter valley and beyond.

# OTTERTON MILL MUSSELS

Take the zest from three of the limes, remove the pith, and chop up the flesh. Put the zest, flesh and juice in a bowl and keep to one side.

Melt the butter and oil together in a large lidded pan. Sauté the onion and garlic until translucent, add the wine, reduce a little and then add the fish stock. Add the lime zest, flesh and juice and the chopped coriander. Check the seasoning.

Throw in the drained mussels.

Put the lid on the pan and cook until the mussels open; this will only take about 5 minutes - any that do not open by then should be discarded.

Add some cream, if necessary, to soften the acidity.

Ladle the mussels into large soup bowls and season with freshly ground black pepper.

Use the remaining lime and some coriander leaves to garnish.

Serve with plenty of Otterton Mill bread.

Mussels are the main fishery on the Exe - there are also cultivated pacific oysters and some wild beds of cockles and clams. Exe mussels are much sought after and grow wild in most areas of the lower Exe estuary. They are sold locally, nationally and also in Europe.

2 lbs/1 kilo of fresh Exe mussels, scrubbed and de-bearded in a bowl of water
4 limes
1 tablespoon of olive oil
1 tablespoon of butter
1 large onion, finely chopped
as many garlic cloves as you like, crushed
5 fl oz/150ml of white wine
5 fl oz/150ml of fish stock
double cream if liked
a large bunch of fresh coriander, chopped (plus a few extra leaves to garnish)
freshly ground black pepper

*There is still a thriving fishing industry in the coastal towns and villages of the East Devon coast. Boats still go out from Exmouth, Budleigh, Sidmouth and Beer and there is plenty of local fish to be had.*

FISH

# FRESH FISH EN CROUTE

Lightly brush a large baking tray with oil. Roll out half the pastry so that it covers the base of the tray. Chill. Heat the oil and about 1oz/25g of the butter in a heavy-based pan and sauté the onion, garlic and mushrooms for a few minutes. Stir in the rice, lemon zest and some herbs.

Season with salt and pepper. Cool. When cool spread the rice mixture over the chilled pastry on the baking tray - leave an edge of pastry showing all the way round.

Put the fish on top of the rice and dot with the rest of the butter. Sprinkle with more herbs and pour the lemon juice all over. Brush beaten egg around the edge of the pastry. Then roll the rest of the pastry out into a rectangle that's a bit larger than the first one and lay it over the top of the fish. Press around the edges well, crimping the pastry into scallop shapes as you go. Cut short, diagonal slits along the top of the parcel. Brush all over with beaten egg and sprinkle with poppy or sesame seeds.

Bake in a pre-heated medium oven until the pastry is golden - about 45 minutes. Serve warm.

This is good with a soured cream and herb sauce.

Serves six to eight people

1lb 8oz/700g puff pastry (preferably, homemade rough puff wholemeal pastry)
1lb 8oz/700g of white fish (pollock, undyed smoked haddock) or salmon, filleted and skinned and cut into chunks
2 tablespoons of sunflower oil
4oz/125g butter
2 onions, peeled and finely chopped
2 cloves of crushed garlic
4oz/125g mushrooms, chopped
4oz/125g cooked rice (we use basmati brown rice but any rice will do)
the juice and zest of a lemon
lots of fresh herbs
sea salt and freshly ground black pepper
a beaten egg to glaze the pastry
poppy or sesame seeds to garnish

# FISH CAKES WITH SAUCE VERTE

Put the fish in a pan and add enough milk to cover it. Gently cook the fish. Allow it to cool, drain and flake it, removing any bones.
Boil the potatoes and when soft, drain them and mash well. Stir in the mayonnaise, and the herbs, the chopped red pepper and the fish. It's important the mixture isn't sloppy.
If it seems so, add a few breacrumbs. Season to taste.
Shape into neat cakes (whatever size you like). Dust with flour, dip into beaten egg, and then roll in breadcrumbs.
Place on a tray and chill for 1 hour before frying in hot oil on both sides. Drain well on kitchen paper and serve with sauce verte.

*i*

1lb/450g white fish (such as cod, whiting, pollack or ling), skinned
enough milk to cover the above in a saucepan
1lb/450g potatoes, peeled and chopped
2 tablespoons of mayonnaise
2 tablespoons each of chopped parsley, chives and dill
1 red pepper, finely chopped
dash of South Devon Chilli Farm Habanero hot sauce (see p116), or Tabasco sauce, or similar
sea salt and freshly ground black pepper
a little flour
a beaten egg
some dried wholemeal breadcrumbs
about 4 tablespoons of sunflower oil

*i* SAUCE VERTE
6 tablespoons of
mayonnaise
1 or 2 cloves of garlic,
peeled and crushed
black pepper
1 bunch of watercress,
washed and chopped
2 tablespoons of parsley,
chopped
2 tablespoons of chives,
chopped
1 tablespoon of basil,
chopped
1 tablespoon of
coriander, chopped
1 tablespoon of tarragon,
chopped
and any other fresh
chopped herbs of your
choice (dill, fennel…)
plus a tablespoon of
chopped capers - if you
like them

Lightly rub the pork all over with some olive oil.

Heat a little more of the oil in a large, heavy-based, roasting pot (one with a tight fitting lid) until it starts to smoke. Add the pork to the pan and turn it until the meat is sealed and is golden brown.

Remove the loin from the pan and put to one side. Pour off some of the excess fat.

Add the cider to the remaining meaty juices - allow it to bubble for a few minutes.

Return the pork to the pan. Add the fennel, tomatoes, haricot beans, garlic, thyme, bay leaf, lemon zest and juice. Sprinkle the fennel seeds over the top and season well.

Bring slowly to the boil. Place the lid firmly on top and allow to simmer gently, over a low heat (or in the oven if you prefer) for 2 to 2½ hours, turning the meat once during this time.

Do not be tempted to speed up the process - the slow cooking makes all the difference

# POT ROAST PORK WITH FENNEL, GARLIC, BEANS & TOMATOES

Enough for six

3 lb/1½ kilos loin of pork - boned, rolled and tied (with rind still on)
some olive oil
1 pint/600ml cider
2 fennel bulbs
about 12 tomatoes, cut in half
8oz/225g dried haricot beans - soaked overnight
16 cloves of garlic, peeled and broken
a sprig of thyme
3 bay leaves
the zest and juice of 1 lemon
2 teaspoons fennel seed, lightly roasted and crushed
sea salt and freshly ground black pepper

# RABBIT IN CIDER WITH PEARS

Heat a little oil in a large heavy-based pan and brown the rabbit pieces; then remove them from the pan and put them to one side. Soften the onion, garlic and celery for a few minutes. Lay the rabbit pieces back in the pan on top of the vegetables. Tuck sprigs of thyme in amongst the meat and then pour over the cider and add enough stock to cover it all. Bring to the boil and then simmer gently until it's cooked – about an hour.

Gently sauté the pear slices in butter, sprinkle over a little brown sugar and let it caramelise.
Stir some of the pears carefully into the casserole before seasoning to taste and serving.
Serve the remaining pears on top.

This is a wonderfully economical casserole that will fill your kitchen with the rich gamey smell of cooking rabbit!
Enough for four to six

some olive oil
2 rabbits, jointed and tossed in flour
2 large onions, chopped
2 to 4 cloves of crushed garlic
4 sticks of celery, chopped
a small bunch of fresh thyme
$\frac{1}{2}$ pint/300ml Jack Ratt's, or similar, local cider (see p100)
enough chicken stock to cover
sea salt and freshly ground black pepper
4 semi-ripe pears, peeled, cored and sliced
a little butter
some brown sugar

MEAT

# CHICKEN & TARRAGON PIE

Pre-heat the oven to a hot setting. Rinse and clean the chicken inside and out and rub it all over with salt, pepper, some of the tarragon and oil. Put the half lemon inside the chicken. Place the chicken, breast down, on a rack in a roasting tin.

Put the chicken into the oven and roast it for 15 minutes. Turn down the oven to a medium setting and roast for a further 30 minutes. Take the roasting tin out of the oven and turn the chicken over. Continue to roast for another 30 to 45 minutes, until the chicken is cooked.

Transfer the chicken to a plate and put to one side.

Drain the fat from the roasting pan into a bowl (keep the roasting juices separate and put to one side).

Transfer a good tablespoon of the fat to a pan, heat, add and sauté the onion, garlic and remaining tarragon. Cook for a few minutes until soft.

Add the wine, the stock and the rest of the roasting juices. Allow to reduce for a few minutes before adding the crème fraiche or soured cream.

Mix the cornflower to a paste with a little water and add it gradually to the sauce until you reach a consistency that you're happy with (not too thick and not too thin) - allow it to bubble a little longer.

Season the sauce to taste and keep warm.

Strip the chicken meat from the bones and cut into even-sized pieces. Put the chicken into an ovenproof dish. (Use the bones to make more stock).

Add any extra juice from the plate that the chicken was resting on to the sauce.

Top the lot off with the rolled out pastry. Once trimmed, scatter sesame seeds and then bake in a moderate oven until golden brown. About 20 minutes.

Serves six to eight

4 lb/2 kilos free-range organic chicken
a good handful of fresh tarragon (or 1 tablespoon of freeze dried)
$\frac{1}{2}$ a lemon
1 onion - chopped finely
2 to 4 cloves of garlic - crushed
a glass of white wine
about $\frac{1}{2}$ pint/300ml of chicken stock
4 tablespoons of soured cream or crème fraiche
2 tablespoons of cornflour
2 tablespoons olive oil
sea salt and freshly ground black pepper
1 lb/450g shortcrust pastry, wrapped in cling film and kept cool in the fridge for about 30 minutes
2 teaspoons of sesame seeds
a beaten egg to glaze

MEAT

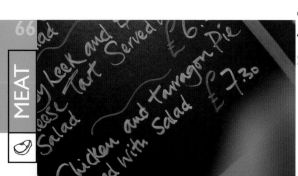

Variations: CHICKEN IN TARRAGON AND CREAM SAUCE (a quicker and easier version) Forget the pastry topping and just serve the dish straight from the pan with fresh spring vegetables.

CHICKEN AND CRANBERRY PIE (a winter seasonal slant) Add about 4 to 6oz/150g of fresh cranberries together with 2oz/50g of chopped and sautéed leeks (instead of the tarragon). Add some double cream (instead of the crème fraiche) to the chicken sauce before the pastry topping is added. A little sugar may also be needed to off-set the sharpness of the cranberries.

CHICKEN AND HAM PIE (a more traditional approach) Try adding about 4 to 6 oz/150g of chopped ham and some fresh thyme (leave out the fresh tarragon).

It's hard to beat a good, well-made pie. Here, in the Mill kitchen, this pie is different every time it's made. It all depends on who's cooking and what seasonal vegetables are in the kitchen. Some ideas for variations are given opposite.

# SPINACH ROULADE

Heat the oil in a heavy-based pan (one with a lid). Add the onion and garlic and soften them for a few minutes - then add the spinach. Cover the pan and cook until the spinach wilts. Drain off any liquid (keep to use as vegetable stock in soups etc.). Stir in the flour, seasoning and nutmeg. Let the mixture cool slightly before stirring in the beaten egg yolks and grated cheese.

Whip the egg whites until they're stiff. Fold them into the mixture.

Pour the mixture into a standard Swiss roll tin lined with baking parchment.

Bake in a medium to low oven for about 20 minutes or until firm to the touch.

Leave to cool for a few minutes before turning onto a sheet of clean baking parchment. Gently peel off the cooking parchment and roll up like a Swiss roll. Leave to cool.

When it's cool, open it up and spread with either cottage cheese or cream cheese - to which you have added some chopped fresh herbs, or finely chopped peppers, or both - and then carefully re-roll.

Makes sufficient to serve six to eight

Serve together with a slice of carrot roulade.

*i*

2 tablespoons of olive oil
1 onion, peeled and finely chopped
2 cloves of crushed garlic
1lbs 8oz/700g fresh organic spinach, washed and finely chopped (frozen works too if well drained)
1 tablespoon of flour
sea salt and freshly ground black pepper
6 eggs, separated
2 tablespoons of grated mature cheddar
lots of freshly grated nutmeg
cottage cheese or cream cheese with some fresh herbs or finely chopped peppers

68

VEG

# CARROT ROULADE WITH WATERCRESS & WALNUT STUFFING

Line a Swiss-roll tray with baking parchment.
Preheat oven to medium.
Melt the butter in a heavy-based pan. Add the grated carrot and cook it until it is soft. Then drain off any liquid, using a colander, and keep to use as stock. Allow the carrots to cool.
When cool add the chopped coriander and the egg yolks.
Season and mix well.
Lay some coriander leaves on the lined Swiss-roll tin and sprinkle the grated cheese evenly on top.
Whisk the egg whites until they form soft peaks and then fold them into the carrot mixture. Spoon the mixture evenly over the cheese in the Swiss-roll tin.
Bake for approx 10 minutes until just firm but not over cooked. Leave to cool for a few moments and then roll it up as for the spinach roulade.

Combine the ingredients for the filling. When the roulade is cool spoon the filling evenly over the surface and roll it up from the short side.

Looks fantastic and tastes brilliant. This is one of Gilly's recipes. She's made it for all sorts of occasions, including the thirteenth wedding anniversary of the Bishop of Tanzania.
Cuts into about six or eight slices - depending on how thick you want them.

3oz/75g butter
1lb 8oz/700g carrots, finely grated
a good-sized bunch of fresh coriander, chopped (plus a few leaves to garnish)
6 eggs, separated
sea salt and freshly ground black pepper
1oz/25g mature cheddar, very finely grated

FOR THE FILLING
2oz/50g walnuts, toasted and chopped
4oz/125g full fat cream cheese
a bunch of watercress, chopped

# BAKED GOAT'S CHEESE & VINE LEAVES WITH ASPARAGUS & BROAD BEAN SALAD

Cut the goat's cheese into 4 small rounds. Put a round of cheese in the centre of each vine leaf and wrap it up like a parcel.

Trim and cook the asparagus until just tender.

Cook the broad beans also until just tender (if they are very fresh and small use them raw).

Mix the olive oil, lemon juice and zest together and then add the tomatoes, black olives and shallots. Season.

Cut the asparagus tips in half lengthways then add them, together with the beans, to the salad and arrange on a plate.

Meanwhile brush the vine leaves with olive oil and bake them in a medium oven for 10 minutes.

While still hot serve with the salad.

We use fresh leaves from the vine in the Mill courtyard. This dish, which serves four, makes a wonderful light lunch. Enjoy it with a glass of crisp wine.

*i*

4 large fresh vine leaves, blanched for 10 minutes and chilled.
5oz/150g Vulscome goat's cheese (or similar log-shaped soft goat's cheese)
1lb/450g young asparagus tips
4oz/125g shelled broad beans
4 tablespoons of olive oil
the juice and zest of a lemon
2 shallots, or 4 spring onions, finely chopped
8 black olives (or more if you like), stoned and halved
6 cherry tomatoes, halved
sea salt and freshly ground black pepper

SALAD

# CAULIFLOWER, CASHEW & CREAM CHEESE SALAD

Put the cauliflower florets in a large open serving bowl. Add the toasted nuts and seeds.

Drizzle over the lemon juice and toss until all the ingredients are lightly coated.

In a small bowl mix the mayonnaise and cream cheese together.

Add the dressing to the cauliflower and mix well.

Season to taste.

For a less rich salad use more mayonnaise and leave out the cream cheese.

This is a delicious salad. Lots of people who don't like cooked cauliflower love this. It's a recipe that Jill came up with years ago.

1 cauliflower, washed and broken into small florets
4oz/125g cashew nuts, toasted until golden brown
2oz/50g pumpkin seeds, toasted until golden brown
1 tablespoon of lemon juice
2 tablespoons of mayonnaise
2 tablespoons of full fat cream cheese
sea salt and freshly ground black pepper

SALAD

# FRESH CARROT, GINGER & APPLE SALAD

In a large bowl combine the carrot, apple, sesame seeds and ginger.
Add the olive oil and stir to coat all the ingredients.
Add the cider and concentrated apple juice and mix again.
Season.

*Using different varieties of apple will vary the flavour of this salad. The fresh ginger should come through the other flavours - don't be afraid to make it a bit hot.*

8oz/225g carrots, finely grated
2 medium-sized eating apples, finely sliced
2oz/50g sesame seeds, lightly roasted
1 heaped tablespoon of fresh ginger, grated
1 tablespoon of olive oil
2 tablespoons of Jack Ratt's, or similar, local cider (see p102) or good quality wine vinegar
1 tablespoon of concentrated apple juice
sea salt and freshly ground black pepper

# FRESH LEMON COLESLAW

Mix the cabbage and apples together in a large bowl. Add the lemon zest and juice. Sprinkle in the raisins and some poppy seeds.
Season.
Stir in the amount of mayonnaise that you like! Serve.

*A lovely fresh salad - better than the usual coleslaw*

a small white cabbage, finely sliced
4 to 6 eating apples (Cox's are ideal), washed, cored and sliced.
the zest and juice of
a lemon
a good handful of raisins
1 tablespoon of poppy seeds
good quality mayonnaise (preferably home made!)
sea salt and freshly ground black pepper

SALAD

In the Middle Ages there were two fulling mills on the mill stream in Otterton. Fulling was the process of cleaning grease out of newly-woven wool cloth and shrinking and tightening the weave. It was a pretty nasty and noisy business. Basically, it involved soaking the cloth in stale urine (villagers got a penny a bucket), slathering it in Fuller's Earth, and endless washing while pounding it with big wooden mallets. The sound (and, presumably, the reek) of a fulling mill would travel quite some distance. After fulling, the cloth would be tucked - that is, stretched - on long wooden frames to which it was attached by L-shaped nails called tenterhooks.

*FULLERS AND TUCKERS PLATE*
*- fish paté served with fresh crusty bread*
*and a selection of salads, washed down*
*with a glass of local ale*

SALAD

# ALMOND MACAROON CAKE

Pre-heat the oven to medium-low
Grease and line a 6 inch spring-form
cake tin.
Cream together the butter and sugar
until light and fluffy. Continue to beat
the mixture as you add the lemon
zest and eggs.
Fold in 4 tablespoons of the crème
fraiche, the sifted flour and the
almonds - if the mixture is too
heavy loosen it by adding the other
tablespoon of crème fraiche.
Bake in the oven for about
30 minutes.
Five minutes before you take the cake
out of the oven make the topping.
Whisk the egg whites until stiff. Add
half the sugar and whisk again. Fold in
the remaining sugar and almonds.
Take cake out of the oven and gently,
but quickly, spread the mixture on the
top. Return the cake to the oven and
cook for a further 20 minutes.
The top should be crisp and
biscuit-coloured.
Cool for 10 minutes and turn out.

Serve warm with spiced plums
(see p43)

*i*

6oz/175g butter
5oz/150g vanilla caster
sugar
the zest of a lemon
2 eggs
4 or 5 tablespoons of
crème fraiche
5oz/150g self-raising flour
3oz/75g ground almonds

2 egg whites
4oz/125g vanilla castor
sugar
3oz/75g ground almonds

SWEET

# CRÈME BRULÉ
# WITH FENNEL OR
# CARDAMOM SEEDS

Split the vanilla pod lengthways. Gently heat the cream in a small pan. Add the vanilla pod and the crushed seeds. Remove from heat and allow to infuse for 30 minutes. Strain through a sieve.

Whisk together the sugar and egg yolks. Then pour in the cream mixture - beating all the time.

Pour this mixture straight into four ramekins and put these into a deep baking dish. Fill the baking dish with boiling water, making sure it doesn't go above the level of the ramekins, and place it in a low oven for 20 minutes or until just set.  Put some damp baking parchment over the baking dish to prevent skin forming on the brûlées.  Chill for at least 2 hours.

Sprinkle with extra sugar and caramelise either with a mini chef blow-torch or under a hot grill.

A perennial favourite with an aromatic twist. For some reason this sweet is always popular at our music nights.
This will make enough for four

*i* 1 vanilla pod
$\frac{1}{2}$ pint/300ml of double cream
1 teaspoon of fennel seeds, crushed (or
1 teaspoon cardamom seeds, crushed)
3 egg yolks
3oz/75g caster sugar

SWEET

# RHUBARB TORTE

This pastry needs to be made at least 12 hours in advance. You will need to use a food processor.

Whiz the sugar, egg and butter together for about 15 seconds. Add the baking powder and flour and whiz again until smooth. Add a little water if necessary.

Tip out and divide in two equal portions. Shape each into a sausage that is about 1½ inches/4cm in diameter (it should fit through the food processor feed tube).

Wrap each pastry sausage in cling film and freeze solid.

One hour before needed remove from the freezer and allow to thaw slightly.

Any fairly sharp fruit works well for this recipe. A plum and apple filling is also given below.

TORTE:
8oz/225g butter
1 egg
4oz/125g light brown sugar
1lb/450g strong white flour
a pinch of baking powder

FRUIT FILLINGS:
RHUBARB AND GINGER
2 lb/900g rhubarb, cut into ½ inch sections
½ inch of fresh ginger
1 to 2 tablespoons of honey (to taste)
1oz/25g butter

*Variation: **PLUM AND APPLE***
*1 lb/450g plums, stoned*
*1 lb/450g dessert apples, peeled and quartered*
*1 or 2 tablespoons of honey (to taste)*
*1oz/25g butter*
*a little water*

Put all the ingredients in a pan and
stew gently until the fruit is soft
(don't overcook rhubarb!). Remove
from the heat.
(Try other fillings - about 2 lb of fruit
is needed which should be cooked to
a loose wet mix).
Grease an 8 inch (preferably loose
bottom) flan tin and line the bottom
with a circle of silicone
baking parchment.
Using the coarse grating disk on the
food processor pass the first of the
two pastry sausages through the
mixer and tip the contents evenly
over the base of the flan tin.
Spread the fruit mix evenly on top.
Grate the second sausage and evenly
spread it on top of the fruit.
Bake in a moderate to hot oven for
about 40 to 50 minutes, until it's
starting to turn a lovely golden colour.

COURTYARD AND TERRACE COME TO LIFE

TARTS, TARTS AND MORE TARTS

TOURISTS, VISITORS, RENEW OLD FRIENDS, HOLIDAYS, SUNTANS

COLD DRINKS AND ICE CREAM

EARLY MORNINGS PREPARING FOR THE RUSH, ADRENALIN

SHORTS, BODIES, BICYCLES

MUSIC FOR A SUMMER EVENING

VIEW FROM PEAK HILL

MOUNTAINS OF WASHING UP AND DIRTY APRONS

POOH STICKS FROM THE BRIDGE

SUDDEN SHOWERS

PEREGRINES HUNTING OVERHEAD AND TAWNY OWLS CALLING

IN THE EVENING

SUMMER

# HONEY & RAISIN SPELT SCONES

Sift the flour, salt and baking powder together into a big bowl. Rub in the margarine with your fingertips until the mixture resembles fine breadcrumbs.

Stir in the honey and raisins and bind the mixture together with just enough milk to form a soft dough. Turn out onto a floured surface and lightly pat down with your hands to form an even layer the depth of your scone cutter (about $1\frac{1}{2}$ to 2 inches). Cut into rounds and place onto a greased baking tray. Brush the tops with beaten egg.

Bake for 30 minutes in the oven at 170°C/Gas mark 3 until golden brown.

*Spelt flour makes really good scones; it's full of flavour and lighter than regular wholemeal flour. Makes about 16 scones*

*i*
1lb 12oz/750g spelt flour
2 dessertspoons of baking powder
6oz/175g margarine
3 dessertspoons of runny honey
4oz/125g raisins
about $\frac{1}{2}$ pint/300ml milk
a beaten egg

*Variation:*
*Use grated apple, raisins and a sprinkle of cinnamon.*
*Make savoury scones with grated cheese, chives and a pinch of chilli.*

80
BAKERY

## Milling and the Millers

*The process of stone grinding flour has remained essentially unchanged since the first mill was built on the Otter. Each set of millstones is made up of a stationary bedstone and a rotating runner stone powered by the waterwheel. The fineness of the flour is controlled by raising or lowering the runner stone.*

*As the grain is crushed, bran, natural oils and vitamins are released and evenly mixed. (A handful of freshly milled flour is warm and smells wonderful.)*

*Milling is done on the first floor and the flour comes down a shute to the ground floor where it is sacked and stored. Millstones grind slowly - it takes 15 minutes to fill a 70lb sack.*

*When Bob and Claire took over the running of Otterton Mill, Claire's father Peter, then 76, temporarily took on the role of millwright. In an effort to find a permanent replacement, a local newspaper wrote an article entitled 'Someone willing to have love affair sought...', and this tempted no fewer than four gallant craftsmen out of the woodwork.*

*Or into it, rather. Brian Hart, Alan Hunt, John Babb and Jerry Tottle - 'The Gang of Four' - are now the Otterton Millers. Three engineers from different backgrounds and a carpenter, enthusiasts for vintage machinery, they had earlier worked as part of a team of volunteers restoring Coldharbour textile mill, near Cullompton.*

*They have extraordinary skills - skills that are fast disappearing.*

*Organic wheat from Tamarisk Farm (see p52) is ground every two or three weeks. When the mill is working it becomes rather like a living thing - the whole building rumbles gently and vibrates to various beats. The millers are aware of every sound, and any change in rhythm has their immediate attention and appropriate response. On milling days visitors can observe the whole fascinating process, and the Gang of Four are always happy to explain what they do. (Make sure you have plenty of time before asking a question, though!)*

## Variation: **CALZONE**

*Make some focaccia dough (right) and divide it in two, then divide each piece into three, giving you six equally sized pieces. Shape the dough pieces into balls and place onto a lightly floured surface.*

*Roll each ball out into a circle about 8 inches/20 cm in diameter. Place the dough circles on trays covered with baking parchment. Spoon whatever filling you want to use down the centre of each circle and then brush the edges of the dough with water.*

*Fold the edges into the centre, one at a time, to form a wrap around the filling. Leave the calzone to prove up for about 20 minutes, or until the dough has started to rise.*

*Bake in a medium oven at 180°C for about 20 minutes (a light bake).*

*While still on the baking trays brush the calzone with olive oil (garlic infused, if possible). When the oil has been absorbed put the calzone onto cooling wires.*

*Calzone are a sort of Mediterranean pasty; a perfect picnic food.*

*We fill our calzone with a ratatouille and feta cheese filling. But you can use a wide variety of others. Many pizza toppings make good fillings (different cheeses, sweated onions, tomatoes, spicy sausage, spinach, peppers…) Or how about using fillets of fish?*

82

# FOCACCIA

Mix all the ingredients together in a large bowl to form a soft dough. Take the dough out of the bowl and knead it for 5 minutes on a lightly floured surface. Return to the bowl, cover and leave until it's almost doubled in size - about 20 minutes. Shape the dough into an oval and place on a baking tray. Drip a little olive oil onto your hand and pat down the surface of the dough to flatten it slightly and to coat it with oil.

Then add some sort of topping like: sweated red onions and peppers, sweated onions and grated cheese, olives and mixed fresh herbs, sliced tomatoes and black pepper, freshly grated lemon with sprigs of rosemary or just plain with coarse salt crystals. Bake in a hot oven at 220°C/Gas mark 7 for about 20 minutes (light bake).

While still on the tray brush with oil, then when the oil has been absorbed put onto a cooling wire.

The name of this bread comes from the Latin word 'focus' meaning fireplace. Long before ovens were used, people along the shores of the northern Mediterranean baked focaccia on the floor of the hearth, in the ashes. Focaccia dough is very versatile. This recipe is for a basic dough, but try adding lemon zest and rosemary to it, or rosemary and garlic, or lemon zest and ground cardamom...

1lb 2 oz/500g unbleached white flour
2oz/50g whole-wheat flour
1oz/25g fresh yeast
$\frac{1}{2}$ a teaspoon of dark brown sugar
1 tablespoon of olive oil
1 egg
$\frac{1}{2}$ pint/300ml lukewarm milk

# COURGETTE & TARRAGON SOUP

Heat the oil and butter in a large heavy-based pan, add the onion, garlic, potato and courgettes and soften well.
Stir in the tarragon and then pour in the vegetable stock. Simmer until just cooked - about 10 to 15 minutes. (Don't overcook because both flavour and colour will be lost).
Blend and season to taste.
Serve with a swirl of cream.

A delicate, light summer soup
Serves four to six

1 tablespoon of sunflower oil
1 tablespoon of butter
2 large onions, peeled and chopped
2 to 4 cloves of garlic, peeled and crushed
1 medium-sized potato, peeled and chopped
6 medium courgettes, chopped
1 tablespoon of freeze-dried tarragon or a bunch of fresh tarragon, chopped
1½ pts/850ml of vegetable stock
sea salt and freshly ground black pepper
a little cream to serve

# PEA & LETTUCE SOUP

Melt the butter in a large heavy-based pan and gently cook the onion for a few minutes. Pour in the stock and add the peas.
Simmer until the peas are tender.
Add the lettuce and the mint and cook until the lettuce has wilted.
Add the milk and blend until smooth.
Reheat and season to taste.
Serve with a swirl of cream or yoghurt and a sprinkle of chopped mint. (This soup is just as good if you use fresh tarragon instead of mint.)

2oz/50g unsalted butter
1 large mild onion, peeled and diced
1 pt/600ml of stock
2 lb/900g of small, tender, young peas
1 head of romaine lettuce, washed and sliced
a large bunch of fresh mint, chopped - keep a little back to garnish
½ pint/300ml of milk
some cream or natural yoghurt
sea salt and freshly ground black pepper

This is based on an Elizabeth David recipe. It's simple to make and absolutely delicious.
Serves six

# TOMATO, BEAN & BASIL SOUP

Heat the oil in a large heavy-based saucepan. Add the onion, carrot, celery, potato, courgettes and garlic and cook gently for 10 minutes, stirring occasionally, until soft and golden.

Add the tomatoes and most of the vegetable stock and simmer until the vegetables are cooked. Add the rest of the stock as necessary.

Blend coarsely.

Add the beans. (If you want to lighten the soup, also add some of the liquid they were cooked in; if not, put it to one side to use as stock later.)

Stir in the pesto to taste and season (perhaps add a little sugar too). Reheat.

Roughly chop the fresh basil and add to the pan just before serving.

Serve with a few whole basil leaves on top to garnish.

At first glance not an obvious choice for summer but the wonderful combination of ingredients provides a delicious and filling lunch which captures the mood of summer afternoons. Serves four to six

4oz/125g haricot beans, soaked overnight and simmered until cooked - about an hour.
2 tablespoons of olive oil
1 large onion, peeled and chopped
2 medium carrots, peeled and chopped
2 sticks of celery, chopped
1 medium-sized potato, peeled, or scrubbed, and chopped
2 courgettes, halved lengthways and sliced
2 to 4 cloves of garlic, peeled and crushed
2 x 400g tins of chopped organic tomatoes
about $1\frac{1}{2}$ pints/850ml of vegetable stock
about a tablespoon of pesto sauce
a large bunch of fresh basil - keep a few leaves to garnish
salt and freshly ground black pepper

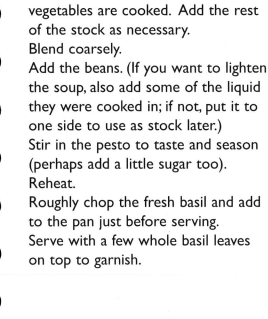

SOUP

# BAKED SPICED SALMON WITH COCONUT & FRESH CORIANDER

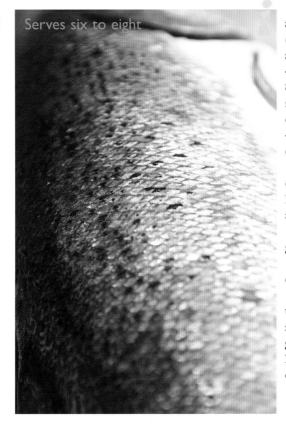

Serves six to eight

Melt the butter in a pan and then add the crushed cardamom seeds and the coconut. Stir continually until the coconut has turned golden brown. Then stir in the chilli, garlic, ginger, ground coriander and turmeric and cook for a further 2 minutes. Season to taste.

Put the salmon into a large roasting tin. Scatter on the fresh coriander, then the dry spice mixture. Cover with cling film and chill for no more than two hours.
Pre heat the oven to a moderately hot setting. Remove the cling film and roast the fish for 10 to 15 minutes until it is just cooked. Serve.
This is good served with raita (yoghurt with finely chopped cucumber and seasoning)

a large side of salmon (about 3 - 4 lbs), skinned and boned
4oz/125g butter
8 green cardamom pods, seeds removed and crushed
4 tablespoons of dried coconut
1 small red chilli, finely chopped
2 garlic cloves, peeled and crushed
1 tablespoon of fresh ginger, finely grated
1 tablespoon of ground coriander
1 heaped teaspoon of turmeric
sea salt and freshly ground black pepper
2 tablespoons of fresh coriander, chopped

FISH

*Topsham nestles on the Exe estuary, between Exeter and the sea. Topsham, like Otterton, was once one of the busiest and most important ports in Devon. From February to August a handful of small boats still go out on the ebb tide fishing for wild salmon.*

Pre-heat the oven to medium-high.
Melt half the butter in a heavy-based
pan and gently sauté the fennel and
celery until soft and golden.
Oil a large baking tray.
Cut squares of baking parchment
big enough to wrap up each fish in
a parcel.
Put a layer of celery and fennel in the
centre of each square of paper and
season with plenty of black pepper
and salt.
Put a large knob of butter and a slice
of orange inside each fish.
Lay the whole fish on top of the fennel
and celery and tuck some more slices
of orange around the edge.
Pour some wine over the top of each
fish - make sure that the vegetables
are moistened.
Pull the edges of the paper together
across the top of the fish and fold and
crinkle them tightly to seal the fish
into its parcel.
Place each parcel on the baking tray
and bake in the oven for about
20 minutes, or until cooked.
Serve in the paper parcels. Pull the
paper open slightly and garnish with
some soft feathery fennel leaves.

# RED MULLET WITH ORANGE & FENNEL IN PARCELS

Individually wrapped in loose
paper parcels, this pretty dish
makes a perfect meal for a
summer dinner party.
Enough for about six parcels.

1 medium-sized mullet
per person, de-scaled
and gutted
4oz/125g butter
2 fennel bulbs, finely
sliced
2 sticks of celery, sliced
2 oranges, peeled and
sliced into rounds
sea salt and freshly
ground black pepper
10 fl oz/300ml of white
wine
baking parchment

# SUMMER BOUILLABAISSE

Clean and prepare the fish. Cut it into large chunks (but leave whole any small fish). Rinse shellfish and prepare the mussels. Always take care to thoroughly scrub fresh mussels under cold, running water and discard any that are open prior to cooking.
Heat the oil in a large heavy-based pan. Gently fry the garlic, onion and celery until soft. Add the tomatoes, herbs and orange zest.
Pour on the hot stock and bring to the boil for 3 to 4 minutes.
Turn down the heat then add the cheaper cuts of fish like coley, ling, rock salmon etc, which will form the main body of the dish. Add some salt with lots of pepper and the saffron. Lay the potato slices over the top and simmer for 10 minutes until the potatoes and fish are nearly cooked. Now add the other fish (the smaller whole fish, pieces of pollock, hake, monkfish, John Dory etc.) which require cooking more gently and carefully to avoid them breaking up completely. Continue to cook for about 6 to10 minutes checking frequently to make sure that the fish is not overcooked.

Serves 8

Add the mussels, prawns and any other shellfish and bring up to heat and cook for 2 to 3 minutes more until the mussels have opened. (Remove any that do not open and throw them away).
Using a perforated spoon, transfer the fish to warmed serving bowls. Pour the remaining liquid over the fish. Garnish with parsley and a large teaspoon of rouille and serve immediately

## ROUILLE
2 to 3 cloves of garlic, crushed into a paste
1 slice of white bread
some fish stock
2 red chilli peppers, chopped very fine
3 tablespoons of olive oil

Moisten the bread with fish stock and mash it together with the garlic. Add the finely chopped chilli peppers. Now add the olive oil drop by drop - beating all the time to make a smooth rich and fiery sauce. (Try adding some roasted, skinned, sweet red pepper - it adds depth to the sauce and gives it a wonderful pink glow).

*i* 3lb/1½ kilos of mixed sea fish such as mullet, rock salmon, gurnard, ling, whiting, John Dory, pollock, coley, hake, monkfish.
8oz/225g shell fish, including mussels and prawns
4 tablespoons of olive oil
3 large cloves crushed garlic
2 onions, chopped
2 sticks of celery, chopped
1lb/450g tomatoes, peeled and chopped
some fresh herbs (thyme, bay leaf, marjoram…)
the zest of an orange
2 pints/1 litre of stock (or water)
sea salt and freshly ground black pepper
½ teaspoon of saffron
2 potatoes, peeled and sliced
a large handful of chopped parsley

91

FISH

# CHICKEN CHERMOULA

Make the chermoula paste first. Gently dry-roast the cumin and coriander seeds, in a frying pan, for a couple of minutes to bring out their flavour. Put to one side. Add half the olive oil to the pan and gently sauté the onions and garlic for a short time.
Then blend or pound with the remaining oil and spices (except the chilli) into a paste using a mortar and pestle or a food processor. Then add chilli to taste.

With the skin side uppermost score the chicken pieces three or four times with a sharp knife. Rub the paste into the chicken and marinate in the fridge overnight in a shallow ovenproof dish covered with cling film.

Serves four

Next day bring the chicken back to room temperature.
Heat the oil in a heavy pan, add the chicken and sear it. Add the vegetables, olives, lemon, honey and dates.
Season with sea salt and black pepper. Add a pinch of cayenne.
Finally, return to the ovenproof dish and add enough boiling stock or water to cover the chicken and vegetables. Cover with foil.
Place the dish in a pre-heated medium-hot oven for 30 to 40 minutes, or until the juices run clear when the meat is pierced.
Chicken Chermoula is wonderful served with couscous that has been steamed in chicken stock. Garnish with natural yoghurt.

4 chicken leg-joints or 8 thighs
4 tablespoons of olive oil
2 carrots, chopped into largish pieces
1 small sweet potato, chopped into chunks
a small handful of black olives, chopped
1 lemon (use a preserved lemon if possible), chopped small
2 tablespoons of runny honey
a handful of stoned fresh dates
sea salt and freshly ground black pepper
a pinch of cayenne
some stock or water

92

*Chermoula is a fresh Moroccan spice paste used as a marinade. Originating from villages in North Africa centuries ago, chermoula means 'the best in the shop' or 'the merchant's best blend'. This is one of Jill's recipes - influenced by the wonderful Claudia Roden. We make our own preserved lemons - well worth the little effort needed.*

*i* FOR THE CHERMOULA
PASTE
1 tablespoon of cumin
seeds
1 tablespoon of
coriander seeds
4 tablespoons of olive oil
2 onions, peeled and
chopped
5 cloves of crushed garlic
1 teaspoon of paprika
$\frac{1}{2}$ to 1 teaspoon of chilli
powder
1 teaspoon of turmeric
a large bunch of fresh
parsley and another of
fresh coriander, chopped
about a teaspoon of
grated fresh ginger
the juice of a lemon

MEAT

# SUMMER LAMB

Mix all the marinade ingredients together in a bowl.
Rub the marinade all over the leg of lamb and leave it covered, in the fridge, for at least an hour.
(Or, preferably, overnight.)
Place the lamb on a rack in a roasting tray and roast for 20 minutes in a hot oven; then turn down to a medium setting and roast for a further $1\frac{1}{2}$ hours.

Meanwhile make the vinaigrette
Whisk the first ingredients together until smooth. Stir in the tomatoes and mint.
Rest the lamb for at least $\frac{1}{2}$ hour before serving warm, thinly sliced, with a drizzle of the vinaigrette.

This is great with local new potatoes tossed in chopped summer herbs and a selection of our salads.
Enough for six to eight

*i*

7 lb/3kilo leg of lamb

MARINADE
2 tablespoons of fresh mint, chopped
2 tablespoons of fresh basil, torn into shreds
2 tablespoons of spring onions, chopped
2 tablespoons of balsamic vinegar
1 tablespoon of olive oil
1 teaspoon of salt
lots of freshly ground black pepper

VINAIGRETTE
6 or 7 tablespoons of olive oil
3 tablespoons of white wine vinegar
2 teaspoons of whole grain mustard
sea salt and freshly ground black pepper
1 dessertspoon of honey
3 tablespoons of fresh mint, chopped
2 ripe tomatoes, chopped

94

MEAT

# WARM ROAST BEEF
# WITH A SALSA VERDE

Rub the beef all over with plenty of salt and pepper.
Heat the oil in a large roasting tray on top of the stove. Put the rib of beef in and seal it in the hot oil for a few minutes.

Sprinkle with the sprigs of fresh thyme and then cook the beef in a hot oven for 15 minutes. Turn the oven down to medium and cook for about another $1\frac{1}{2}$ hours for medium-rare
(add another 15 minutes for medium, or add 30 minutes for medium to well done).
While it's cooking baste the beef, every so often, with any juices in the pan. If the bottom of the pan seems a little dry, add some beef stock or water.

Leave the meat to rest for 30 minutes. Carve and serve with a drizzle of salsa verde

Never compromise on the quality of the beef. Always seek out your local supplier of meat from naturally fed and reared stock - you will taste the difference.
Enough for four to six

*i*

a rib of beef on the bone
(about $3\frac{1}{2}$ lb/ $1\frac{1}{2}$ kilos)
sea salt and freshly
ground black pepper
a little olive oil
sprigs of fresh thyme

SALSA VERDE
2oz/50g fresh mint
2oz/50g parsley
2oz/50g fresh basil
2 tablespoons of green capers
4 tablespoons of olive oil
1 garlic clove, peeled and crushed
1 teaspoon of mustard
4 to 6 fillets of anchovy (optional)
sea salt and freshly ground black pepper.

Blend all the ingredients in a food processor, adding more oil if needed.

MEAT

# ROASTED FILLED SWEET PEPPERS

Oil the cut halves of the peppers and place them onto a roasting tin. Bake them in a hot oven for 10 minutes until they've softened.

Put the couscous into a deep bowl and pour 6 tablespoons of boiling water onto it and add the knob of butter. Put it to one side.

Heat the remaining oil in a pan and cook the spring onions and the mushrooms for a few minutes.

Add the tomatoes and half the fresh herbs. Cook gently, until the tomatoes have softened, then add the couscous and the rest of the fresh herbs.

Fill each of the roasted pepper halves with the mixture and top with a circle of goat's cheese.

Return to the hot oven and bake for a further 10 to 15 minutes until the cheese is melting and starting to brown.

Serves four

4 large red peppers, halved and de-seeded
4 tablespoons of olive oil
4oz/125g couscous
a knob of butter
a bunch of spring onions, chopped
5oz/150g mushrooms, sliced
4oz/125g cherry tomatoes, halved
a handful of fresh mint, finely chopped
a small handful of fresh coriander, finely chopped
6oz/175g mild creamy goat's cheese such as Vulscombe (see p35), cut into 4 rounds

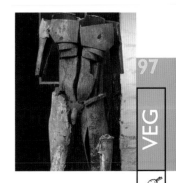

97

VEG

# ROASTED RED ONION & GOAT'S CHEESE TART

Put all the onions onto a baking tray, drizzle with plenty of olive oil, and place in a hot oven.

Roast for about 10 to 15 minutes until they've softened and started to brown at the edges. Sprinkle with balsamic vinegar and put back in the oven for another 10 minutes.

While the onions are still hot season them with plenty of cracked black pepper and a little salt. Stir in the honey and three-quarters of the basil. Spoon the roasted onions over the base of the tart.

Mix the eggs and cream together in a bowl, then pour the mixture over the onions.

Lay slices of goat's cheese on top and sprinkle with the remaining basil.

Place gently into a medium oven and cook for 25 to 35 minutes until just firm but still slightly wobbly in the centre.

Because these tarts are open they must look great. The ingredients have to be fresh and colourful. As Sarah says 'You've got to be able to eat them with your eyes.'

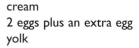

Basic tart blind baked (see p20)
6 medium red onions, cut into chunks
some olive oil
1 tablespoon of balsamic vinegar
1 tablespoon of runny honey
sea salt and cracked black pepper
2 handfuls of torn basil leaves
$\frac{1}{2}$ pint/300ml double cream
2 eggs plus an extra egg yolk
6oz/175g Vulscombe goat's cheese (see p35), or similar

98

# COURGETTE, FETA & TARRAGON TART

Melt the butter in a heavy-based pan and sauté the courgettes for 10 minutes. Add the spring onions and tarragon and cook for a few more minutes until the courgettes begin to go slightly brown at the edges

Put the vegetables into the cooked pastry case and cover with the crumbled cheese.

Combine the eggs and cream in a bowl and season; pour this mixture over the vegetables.

Bake the tart in a moderate oven for 25 to 30 minutes until the filling is set but still slightly wobbly in the centre.

Basic tart, blind baked (see p20)
2oz/50g butter
8oz/225g courgettes, sliced into thin rounds
a small bunch of spring onions, finely chopped
a handful of chopped tarragon leaves
2 eggs plus an extra egg yolk
$\frac{1}{2}$ pint/300ml double cream
sea salt and freshly ground black pepper
6oz/175g of crumbled 'Ridgewell Original' cheese (or similar feta-style cheese)

*LADIES WHO LUNCH PLATE*
*Otterton Mill tart served with a selection of*
*salads and a glass of English Country Wine*
*(see following pages)*

99

### Our country wines people: The Lyme Bay Winery at Shute

*It's not unusual - allegedly - for stockbrokers to turn to drink; few, however, can have done it as successfully as Nigel Howard. Thirteen years ago, he quit the City, returned to his native West Country, and started brewing cider. Why cider?*

'Well, it's my favourite drink. And I wanted to do something that had a real end-product, something you could hold in your hand and say 'I made that'. The mass-produced stuff is terrible, and I thought there was a market for quality. And I happened to know Julian Temperley, the great Somerset cider maker, who gave me lots of help and advice.'

*He set up in a farm not far from Seaton.* 'It was a lovely old place - the kind of place that tourists think real cider should come from. But it wasn't very practical. Cider is actually quite a delicate and complex drink. All sorts of things can vary its quality, and at 5% alcohol it's not robust enough to deal with the wrong sorts of bacteria. And the farm, well, the roof leaked, we had rats...'

*So there's no truth in the old story about rats being useful to the cider-maker, about popping one into the brew?*

'Well,' *Nigel says, cautiously,* 'there is an element of truth there. Meat proteins can aid the clarifying process. In the old days, people did drop in a bit of bacon or something. Our own cider is called Jack Ratt, partly as a joke about all that. Honest.'

*After two years contentedly making cider in his lovely unsuitable farm, Nigel had to confront the fact that he wasn't making any money. So he turned his mind to traditional, fruit-based country wines and fruit liqueurs; and the business grew. Five years ago, he moved to the present winery, which is a big, purpose-built plant overlooking a great swathe of East Devon countryside that falls in slow folds towards the Axe estuary. Here, gleaming technology meets pure and simple ingredients, and the results are displayed in the Winery shop. There are now thirty-two country wines, a spectrum of lovely colours in their clear glass bottles; slender bottles of fruit liqueurs; organic cordials; glass and stoneware flagons of Jack Ratt; sparkling cider; cider vinegar; dark, long-necked bottles of cream liqueurs; cider brandy; jars of chutneys and preserves.*

*The winery is a growing (and award-winning) project; we asked Nigel how he sees it developing.* 'Well, you have to grow, just to stand still. But you have to be careful not to lose sight of what you're trying to do, your identity. We've been approached by supermarket buyers, but we won't go down that route. For one thing, it would compromise our service to our network of independent outlets like the Mill. Plus we produce our wines in relatively small batches, and we like to experiment with new products. I wouldn't want to be told what to make and how. Apart from all that, we're still a small business, just ten permanent staff as well as myself and Mark, the Brewer.*

*It's got a family feel to it. We all know how things work, and can do a bit of everything. Like on a day in late spring, when the blossom is just right and the weather is perfect, we all down tools and go out gathering elderflowers. I'd hate to be so busy that we couldn't do that. What would be the point?'

# OTTERTON MILL GREEK-STYLE SUMMER SALAD

## SALAD

8oz/225g small cherry tomatoes, halved
1 cucumber, seeded, quartered lengthways and chopped into 2 inch/5cm lengths
1 small red onion, chopped finely
3 spring onions, chopped
1 tablespoon of fresh coriander, roughly chopped
1 red pepper, diced
1 cos lettuce, or 2 little gem lettuces, shredded
a small bunch of fresh flat-leafed parsley, chopped
sea salt and freshly ground black pepper
1 whole fresh Tiverton 'Ridgewell Original' cheese (or about 6oz/175g of other feta-style cheese), crumbled
10 pitted black Greek olives

Combine the ingredients and add the dressing.
Pile onto plates and eat with fresh rosemary and lemon focaccia bread hot from the oven.
Add a glass or two of wine and eat outside in the sunshine!

## DRESSING

3 tablespoons of olive oil
4 teaspoons of lemon juice
a large bunch of fresh oregano and marjoram, chopped
sea salt and freshly ground black pepper

Combine all the ingredients and chill.

102

## TOMATO & FRESH BASIL SALAD

Put all the ingredients into a serving dish. Drizzle with olive oil and toss together.
Pour on the dressing, mix again, and serve with fresh hot bread.

SALAD INGREDIENTS
2 large handfuls of fresh basil, torn
1lb 8oz/700g cherry tomatoes, chopped in half (or the same quantity of ripe tomatoes, sliced or cut into wedges)
8 - 10 black olives

DRESSING
2 tablespoons of balsamic vinegar
6 tablespoons of olive oil
1 tablespoon each of chopped parsley, mint and basil
1 teaspoon of Highfield's sundried tomato whole seed mustard (or similar good quality mustard)
salt and freshly ground black pepper
Combine all the ingredients in a small lidded jar and shake well.

## NEW POTATO SALAD WITH SPRING ONIONS & FRESH HERBS

Scrub the potatoes and then cook them in salted, boiling water
(or steam them).
Coat the warm
potatoes with the oil, lemon juice and seasoning.
When they're cool add the spring onions, lemon zest and fresh herbs.
(You may need to add some extra oil as the warm potatoes absorb it readily).
Serve.

1lb/450g new potatoes
3 tablespoons of olive oil
sea salt and cracked black pepper
a large bunch of spring onions, chopped finely
the zest and juice of a lemon
a large bunch of your favourite fresh herbs, finely chopped

SALAD

### Our ice cream people: Jane and Jamie Marsh of Rookbeare Farm

More than a few people have had mind-altering experiences at the Glastonbury Festival. Jane and Jamie had theirs in 1989. It had nothing to do with Van Morrison, and the only enchanting substance involved was ice cream. Their own ice cream, made with the milk from their small herd of Jersey cows.

'The funny thing is,' Jamie says, 'that we didn't want to go. We'd already done the Devon County Show and one or two other events, and selling ice cream in dodgy weather without a reliable electricity supply had started to lose its charms. But we were persuaded to do it. As it turned out, the weather was wonderful, and we had a queue forming before we'd finished setting up. At the end of the first day we'd sold out, and had to make an overnight dash back to Devon to restock. By the end of the festival we were thinking 'Yeah, we might just be able to make a go of this.'

Jane and Jamie bought Rookbeare Farm in 1983. It wasn't good timing. Almost as soon as they'd got up and running they were hit by a double whammy: the introduction of milk quotas, then the butter-fat regulations. Basically, that meant that they couldn't expand their herd, and couldn't make a living bulk-selling high-quality milk. They had to diversify. 'Jersey milk isn't ideal for cheese, so we went for ice cream. The fact that it's one of my favourite things in the world - and still is - may have had something to do with it.

106

*So we took a load of our milk down to Seal Hayne College and persuaded them to let us have the run of their ice cream kitchen for a day. That's how we started.'*

*We go across to 'the factory', a barn that occupies one whole side of the yard.*

*'We've only recently managed to bring the whole process under one roof. Now the whole thing, the kitchen, the labelling and packing, the storage freezers, is in here. It's great; we spent years lugging stuff from one part of the farm to another.'*

*In the kitchen, Jane, with a single helper, is filling tubs with mango and passion fruit ice cream; it comes out of a big tap like a thick golden rope. Jane is a petite person, but on this sub-zero day she's swaddled in so many layers beneath her white overall that she looks like a Beryl Cook lady dressed for bowls.*

*'It all looks a bit high-tech,' she says, gesturing at the array of shiny steel vats and pipework, 'but it's dead simple. Fresh milk goes in one end, then goes through the homogeniser, which disperses the cream through the milk so that it doesn't separate when it's frozen. Next, we add the other ingredients - the free range eggs, the cane sugar, the fruit, our home-made fudge, or whatever - and then it's chilled and comes out here. That's it.'*

*It's not always easy to keep things simple. In the early days, when the Marshs were seeking expert advice, they were told that you had to use fruit syrups, stabilizers, anti-oxidants; it just wouldn't work otherwise. The experts were wrong, and Jane and Jamie were right. It's not only bombed-out festival goers who think so; Rookbeare ice cream is now available at Waitrose (as well as Otterton Mill).*

*Back in the (thank God) warm farmhouse kitchen Jamie says 'We're not evangelical about organics or anything. It's just that for us, the best stuff happens to be what's been least mucked about with. Like the Havana Club rum we use in our daiquiri sorbets. We discovered it on a trip to Cuba. Most rum is horrible, really. But Havana Club is fabulous simply because the way they produce it hasn't changed in over a hundred years. The process has hardly been industrialised at all. They're a bit backward over there.' He smiles. 'We can relate to that.'*

# OPEN-FACED APRICOT & ROASTED HAZELNUT TART

Arrange the apricots around the pastry case and scatter with hazelnuts.
Combine the eggs, honey and cream and pour over the fruit and nuts in the tart.
Place in a moderate oven and bake for 20 to 30 minutes until the tart has just set.

Serve these open tarts warm with a good scoop of Rookbeare Farm ice cream - or a similar good quality local ice cream.

9 inch/22cm baked sweet pastry case (see p40)
6-8oz/175-225g fresh, ripe apricots, halved and stoned
3oz/75g whole hazelnuts, roasted and roughly chopped
3 eggs
1 tablespoon of honey
$\frac{1}{2}$ pint/300ml double cream

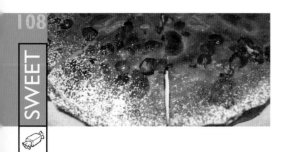

SWEET

# OPEN-FACED GOOSEBERRY & HONEY TART

Combine the egg yolks, cream and honey.
Arrange the gooseberries attractively in the baked pastry case.
Pour over the cream and egg mixture. Place in a moderate oven and bake for 20 to 30 minutes until the tart is just set.

(Elderflower combines wonderfully with gooseberries. If you can find some pick a head, wash it and strip the flowers from the stalks, and add to the cream mixture.)

9 inch/22cm baked sweet pastry case (see p40)
8oz/225g fresh gooseberries, washed, topped and tailed
3 tablespoons of runny honey
2 eggs
$\frac{1}{2}$ pint/300ml double cream

Grease an 8 inch/20cm loose-based flan tin and line the bottom with a circle of silicone baking parchment. Finely crumb the shortcake and press into the flan tin, taking it very slightly up the edges.

Chill for quarter of an hour.

Put 4oz/125g of the fudge and the 2 tablespoons of cream into a bowl and melt in a microwave or using a bain-marie. Pour over the shortcake base. Put into the fridge to reset the fudge.

Next put the cream cheese, cream, eggs, vanilla and sugar in a bowl and beat until smooth.

Pour the mix into the cooled flan base. Bake in a moderate to low oven for an hour, or until the edges are browning slightly.

(The mixture should have started to firm but still be slightly wobbly in the centre. If it browns too quickly cover with greaseproof paper and lower the oven temperature a little.)

Switch the oven off and leave the cake in the cooling oven for a further hour; this will help to prevent it from cracking.

Place the rest of the fudge and 2 teaspoons of water in a small bowl and melt in the microwave or in a bain-marie. Dribble, drag or comb the melted fudge onto the cheesecake in an Abstract Expressionist (!) style. Cool and then serve.

# JACKSON POLLOCK STYLE DEVON FUDGE CHEESECAKE

One 7oz packet of Otterton Mill plain shortcake

FILLING
6oz/175g Devon fudge
1lb/450g full fat cream cheese
4 fl oz/120ml double cream plus 2 extra tablespoons
3 large eggs
1 vanilla pod, split open, and the insides scraped out
4oz/125g golden sugar

SWEET

# STRAWBERRY COCONUT FLAN

Lightly oil an 8 inch/20cm loose-based flan tin.
Mix together the almonds, coconut, sugar and melted butter.
Press the mixture firmly into the prepared tin.
Bake in a medium oven for 12 to 15 minutes. Cool.

Beat together the cheese, sour cream, sugar, lemon rind and juice until smooth.
Spread evenly over base and arrange the strawberries over the top.

This simplest of sweet flans requires the minimum of cooking and preparation.

4oz/125g ground almonds
4oz/125g shredded coconut
1oz/25g brown sugar
2oz/50g melted butter
8oz/225g low fat cream cheese
2 tablespoons of sour cream
4oz/125g light brown sugar
the grated rind and juice of a lemon
8oz/225g strawberries

SWEET

AUTUMN

# BUTTERNUT SQUASH WALNUT BREAD

Put the squash into saucepan of water and bring to boil. Cook for about 20 minutes, or until tender. Drain well and then blend into a paste, allow to cool.

Put 10oz/275g of the butternut paste into a bowl. Add the sugar, butter, nutmeg and eggs and mix together. Sift the flour, salt and baking powder together, make a well in the centre, and add the butternut mix and the walnuts. Fold together until smooth. Line and oil a 2 lb loaf tin with baking parchment and tip the mixture in. Bake at approximately 170°C/Gas mark 3 for about 40 minutes until golden brown, shrinking from the sides of the tin and firm to the touch.

1lb/450g butternut squash, peeled, de-seeded and cut into chunks
3oz/75g dark brown sugar
2oz/50g melted butter
1 teaspoon of ground nutmeg
4 eggs
1lb/450g wholemeal flour
$\frac{1}{2}$ teaspoon of salt
1 or 2 teaspoons of baking powder
3oz/75g chopped walnuts

# LYDIA'S 'FREE FROM' MOIST FRUIT CAKE

Grease and line a 2 lb loaf tin.
Put the flour, baking powder, bicarbonate of soda and the spices into a large bowl.
Put all the other ingredients into a stainless steel saucepan and bring gently to the boil. Reduce the heat and stir well. Simmer for 5 minutes. Take pan away from heat and leave to cool.
Pour the cooled mixture into the dry ingredients and stir until thoroughly mixed. Spoon the mixture into the prepared loaf tin.
Bake for 45 to 50 minutes at 200°C/Gas mark 6 until firm.

This cake is perfect for anyone who has any allergies to eggs, wheat, sugar, dairy products or nuts.
It's a really tasty cake that is very similar to a moist malt loaf in flavour and texture.

10oz/275g rye flour
1 teaspoon of baking powder
1 teaspoon of bicarbonate of soda
$\frac{1}{2}$ teaspoon of cinnamon
$\frac{1}{2}$ teaspoon of cloves
$\frac{1}{2}$ teaspoon of nutmeg
3oz/75g grated carrot
6oz/175g chopped dates
6oz/175g raisins
1 dessert apple, grated
the zest of an orange
$12\frac{1}{2}$ fl oz/360ml water
1 tablespoon of concentrated apple and pear spread (available in most health food shops)

115

BAKERY

**Our chilli people: Steve and Jason of the South Devon Chilli Farm near Loddiswell**

The very words 'South Devon chilli farm' sound pretty unlikely; one of those joke phrases like 'Norfolk Mountain Rescue.' And your first sight of the place does little to dispel scepticism: a big steel-sided agro-shed perched on the side of an undulating green valley in the South Hams. Then you step inside and the aromas hit you; dried and smoked chillies can and do smell like banana, freshly-cured tobacco, lemon, chocolate...

The chillies grow in big poly-tunnels ranged along the south-facing slope of the valley. Steve and Jason give us a tour, rattling off names; there are more than eighty varieties from Latin America, the Caribbean, Asia. The plants are extraordinarily varied in size and shape, as are the fruit: dangerous-looking thin red ones, big crinkly green ones, innocent-seeming pale yellow ones, others that look like cherries or tomatoes. We're particularly struck by two spectacularly beautiful varieties called Twilight and Rainbow which have little, cone-shaped, multicoloured fruits - scarlet, yellow, pink and mauve - growing from a single stem. 'We sell a lot of those as ornamental houseplants,' Steve says.

Trying to sound horticultural, we ask if growing these exotic things in south Devon is risky, in terms of pests and diseases. 'Luckily no,' Jason says, 'because we're organic growers, and we don't and won't use pesticides. Actually, our biggest problem is mice and voles. It turns out that they're very fond of chillies.'

Which surprises us. Makes you wonder what the local owls make of chilli-flavoured voles.

This is Steve and Jason's fourth season on the present site, and they are very successful. That's official; in 2005 they were in the HSBC's top ten successful new small businesses. And their produce - not just the dried chillies, but also the jellies, jams and sauces - have gathered a hatful of prizes. Their Hot Habanero Sauce won Gold in the National Great Taste Awards, which means that it's probably the best chilli sauce in the country.

You can find their range of products at farmers' markets throughout the region, and, of course, at the Mill. Or, if you fancy spicing up a day out in the South Hams, try this: call in at the chilli farm, buy a Rainbow and stock up on the hot stuff (don't forget their wonderful chilli chocolate), drive to the coast, buy a portion of chips and slap on the Thai chilli sauce. Fantastic. You won't mind that it's raining.

116

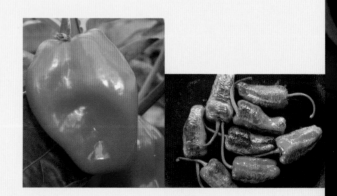

# TRADITIONAL GINGERBREAD

Grease and line a 12 inch/30cm cake tin.
Put all the dry ingredients into a large bowl and mix together.
Warm the milk.
Melt the margarine with the golden syrup and the treacle in a saucepan over a low heat. When they're all runny and melted together take the pan away from the heat and add the milk and the beaten eggs. Stir well.
Tip this mixture into the bowl of dried ingredients and mix well.
Pour the mixture into the prepared cake tin and bake in the centre of the oven at 150°C/Gas mark 2 for about 1 hour. Check to see if the gingerbread is cooked by pressing the top of the cake which should spring back into shape when it's ready.

This is a fabulous all-year-round cake. Hot and spicy with a lovely rich colour, it's a permanent favourite in the restaurant and in the shop.
Gingerbread keeps really well provided it's wrapped and kept somewhere cool in an airtight container.

1lb/450g whole-meal flour
8oz/225g light brown sugar
$\frac{1}{2}$ teaspoon of bicarbonate of soda
1 teaspoon of ground ginger
1 teaspoon of mixed spice
$\frac{1}{2}$ teaspoon of salt
8oz/225g organic margarine
8oz/225g golden syrup
8oz/225g black treacle
3 eggs, beaten
$\frac{1}{2}$ pint/300ml milk

119

BAKERY

# BUTTERNUT SQUASH, APPLE & ROASTED RED PEPPER SOUP

Enough for 6 hearty servings

De-seed, skin and chop the butternut squash into large chunks. Put the squash in a baking tray with the apples and add water or stock to a depth of about $\frac{1}{2}$ inch. Bake in a fairly hot oven until softened - about 30 minutes.

Melt the butter in large pan over a low heat. Add the onions and allow them to sweat for a couple of minutes. Then add the celery, carrots, cinnamon and the fresh mixed herbs and cook slowly until soft. Gently warm the vegetable stock.

Sprinkle the flour over the cooked vegetables and then add the heated stock, stirring well to avoid lumps.

Add the roasted butternut squash and apples to the pan and stir in. Blend.

Season to taste.

Add most of the cream and the chopped red peppers - keep back just enough to garnish.

Serve with a swirl of cream and a scattering of peppers (or a swirl of pepper puree).

1 large (or 2 medium sized) butternut squash
1 lb/450g bramley apples, peeled, cored and chopped in half
2oz/50g butter
4oz/125g onions, chopped
4oz/125g carrots, chopped
half a head of celery, chopped
$\frac{1}{2}$ teaspoon of cinnamon
a small handful of mixed fresh herbs (rosemary, thyme, marjoram…)
$1\frac{1}{2}$ pints/850ml of vegetable stock
2oz/50g wholemeal flour
sea salt and freshly ground black pepper
4 tablespoons of double cream
2 large red peppers, roasted, skinned, de-seeded and very finely chopped (or even blended to a puree)

SOUP

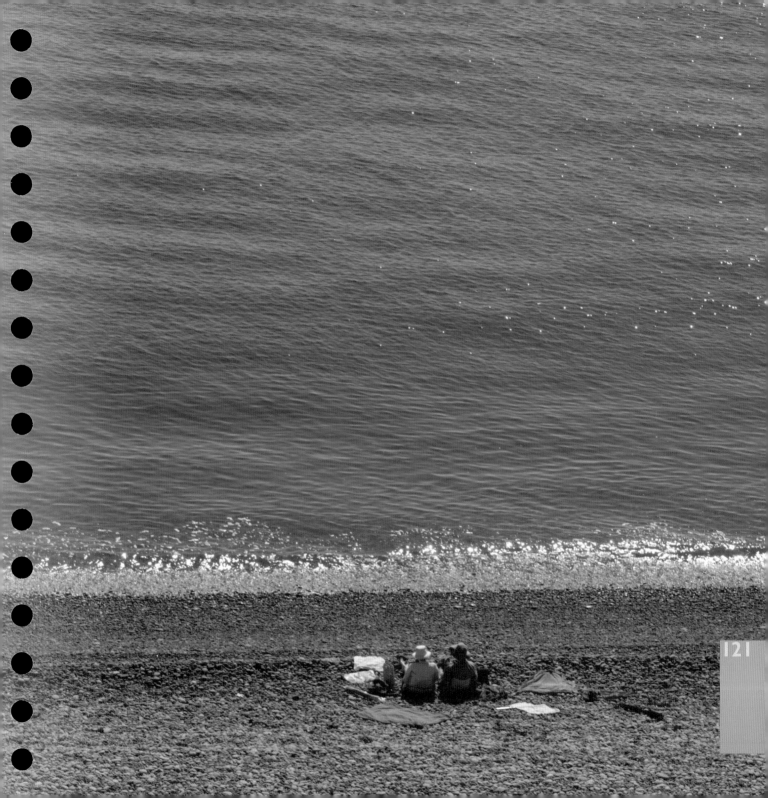

121

# LENTIL, GINGER & LEMON SOUP

Heat the oil in a large heavy-based saucepan over medium heat. Add the onion, carrot, celery and garlic and sauté them for a few minutes until they soften. Add the ginger. Stir in the lentils and cover with the vegetable stock.

Halve the lemon; cut one half into 4 and add the segments to the soup.

Bring the soup to the boil and simmer until the vegetables and lentils are cooked - about 20 to 30 minutes.

Cool slightly and blend.

Season to taste with salt, pepper, lemon juice (from the remaining half lemon) and more grated ginger. The consistency may also need adjusting. Stir in freshly chopped coriander to serve.

A warming, tangy, winter soup. A good basic lentil soup provides you with opportunity for endless variation. By adding different herbs, spices, vegetables and even fruit in varying proportions you could make a new soup for almost every day of the year. The only limitation is your imagination

Serves 4

*i*

2 tablespoons of olive oil
1 large onion, peeled and chopped
2 large carrots, peeled and sliced
4 sticks of celery, chopped
2 to 4 cloves of garlic, peeled and crushed
about. 2oz/50g of fresh ginger, peeled and grated
4oz/125g red lentils
2 pints/1 litre of hot vegetable stock
1 lemon
salt and freshly ground black pepper
fresh coriander to garnish

SOUP

# PUMPKIN & APPLE SOUP

Heat the oil in a large saucepan; add the onions and the garlic and cook for a couple of minutes. Then add the pumpkin, apples and sage. Cook for another couple of minutes until softened. Season well and add the stock and the cider or apple juice. Bring to the boil and simmer for 15 to 20 minutes until the vegetables are tender.
Blend. Check seasoning.
Serve piping hot with crusty bread.

Enough for four to six people

*i* 2 onions, peeled and chopped
1 clove garlic, peeled and crushed
1 tablespoon of olive oil
1lb/450g pumpkin, skinned, seeded and cubed
2 sharp cooking apples, peeled, cored and chopped
1 pint/600ml vegetable stock
$\frac{1}{2}$ pint/300ml Luscombe Farm dry cider or apple juice, or similar (see p150)
2 sprigs of fresh sage
sea salt and freshly ground black pepper

SOUP

# MUSHROOM & WALNUT SOUP

Heat the oil and butter in a heavy-based pan (one with a lid) and soften the onions, garlic and potato. Add the mushrooms, stir, put the lid on the pan and leave them to soften for a few minutes.

Pour in the warm stock and simmer for 10 to 15 minutes until all the vegetables are tender.

Add the toasted walnuts and lightly blend - leave some texture.

At this point (when cooled slightly) add the cream, milk or yoghurt. If using yoghurt you may choose not to add lemon juice.

Season to taste.

A dash of soy sauce helps to bring out the mushroom flavour.

Serve with a swirl of cream and a sprinkling of toasted broken walnuts.

Enough for four to six

This is one of Jill's recipes and one of her very favourite soups. The walnuts make it really special.

1 tablespoon of sunflower oil
a little butter
2 large onions, peeled and chopped
2 to 4 cloves of crushed garlic
1 large potato, peeled and chopped
1lb 8oz/700g mushrooms, washed and roughly chopped
3 to 4oz/100g of toasted broken walnuts (walnuts have a very strong flavour so use more or fewer nuts depending on your taste)
about 2 pints/1 litre of warm vegetable stock
sea salt and freshly ground black pepper
a little lemon juice
a dash of soy sauce
$\frac{1}{4}$ pint/150ml double cream, milk or thick yoghurt
a few broken walnuts toasted for a garnish

SOUP

# SMOKED HADDOCK & LEEK TART

Melt the butter in a heavy-based pan and sauté the leeks for 15 to 20 minutes. Don't overcook them; they should be still firm.
Put the haddock in a wide shallow pan and pour over enough milk to just cover it and simmer until the fish is just cooked.
Drain the fish. Remove the skin and flake the flesh.
Put the flaked fish and the leeks into the cooked pastry case.
Combine the eggs and cream and season well, then pour over the leeks and fish.
Bake in a moderate oven for 25 to 30 minutes until the tart is set but is still slightly wobbly in the middle.

A scrumptious tart!

Basic tart, blind baked (see p20)
10oz/275g naturally smoked haddock
1lb/450g leeks, chopped into $\frac{1}{2}$ inch rings
2oz/50g butter
a little milk
a small bunch fresh dill
sea salt and freshly ground black pepper
2 eggs plus 1 extra egg yolk
$\frac{1}{2}$ pint/300ml double cream

FISH

Heat the oil in a heavy-based pan and fry the onions until they're soft. Add the garlic, ginger and the spices and fry gently for a few more minutes to release the flavours. Add the tomato puree and chopped tomatoes and stir in.

Cover with water and heat until simmering. Add the creamed coconut and simmer for a further 10 to 15 minutes until the coconut has completely melted.

Add the lemon juice and salt and pepper to taste.

The curry can now stand for some time and rest until you are ready to use it.

About 10 minutes before you want to eat, bring the curry up to boiling and then lower the heat. When the curry is simmering add the fish and cook for about 10 minutes until the fish is ready, then add the prawns. Bring back up to full heat and simmer for a further 2 to 3 minutes.

Serve with rice and a large spoonful of organic plain yoghurt. Sprinkle some chopped coriander over the top.

# GHURKHA FISH & PRAWN CURRY

This recipe has been in Sarah's family longer then she cares to remember. It originally came from a relative who served in India and who befriended a ghurka whilst out there.
Serves four to six

1lb/450g firm fish such as rock salmon
8oz/225g fresh prawns, shells removed
2 tablespoons of sunflower oil
4 onions, chopped in half and then quartered and then separated
3 cloves of garlic, peeled and crushed
1 inch/3 cm of fresh ginger, finely grated
4 dessertspoons of ground coriander
2 dessertspoons of ground cumin
1 teaspoon of turmeric
a stick of cinnamon
$\frac{1}{2}$ teaspoon of fresh red chilli, finely chopped
$\frac{1}{2}$ of a tube of tomato paste
5 medium tomatoes, chopped
$\frac{1}{2}$ of a block of creamed coconut, broken into pieces
juice of half a lemon
sea salt and freshly ground black pepper
handful of coriander, coarsely chopped

# BOBOTIE

Serves six to eight

Pre-heat the oven to medium.
In a heavy-based pan heat the oil
and sauté the onions and garlic
until they soften and turn a light
golden-brown.
Add and gently fry the ginger,
turmeric, ground spices and
almonds for a few minutes. Then
add the meat and brown it.
While the meat is browning soak
the breadcrumbs in a little
milk - then squeeze and crumble
the wet bread into the pan.
Finally add the stock, chutney,
apricots and herbs and cook for a
further 2 minutes. Turn mixture
into a prepared dish and bake in
the oven for 45 minutes.

Combine the eggs with the sour
cream and yoghurt and whisk. Pour
over the meat. Arrange the bay
leaves on top and put the dish
back in the oven until set
- about 20 minutes.
Good served with rice.

2lb/900g minced beef
a little olive oil
2 medium onions, peeled
and chopped
2 cloves of garlic, peeled
and crushed
2 teaspoons of fresh
ginger, grated
1 teaspoon of turmeric
1 tablespoon of freshly
ground coriander
1 tablespoon of freshly
ground cumin
2oz/50g flaked almonds
2oz/50g fresh bread
crumbs
a little milk
$\frac{1}{4}$ pint/150ml beef stock
or water
4 tablespoons of
Highfield's West Country
Cider Chutney (or similar
very fruity chutney)
a handful of fresh mixed
herbs
a large handful of fresh
coriander, chopped
3oz/75g sharp dried
apricots, soaked and
chopped
2 eggs, beaten
4 tablespoons of sour
cream
4 tablespoons of organic
natural yoghurt
6 bay leaves

MEAT

*Africa is a continent full of flavours - many brought from different lands and cultures. Bobotie came to South Africa via Malaysia sometime in the 17th century. It is a kind of spicy exotic shepherd's pie that is still a traditional dish throughout many parts of Africa.*

# PORK TERRINE

Serves six to eight

1lb 8oz/700g lean pork
1lb/450g belly pork
8oz/225g pig's liver
8oz/225g streaky bacon
6 large cloves of garlic,
finely chopped
grated zest and juice of a
lemon
grated zest and juice of an
orange
$\frac{1}{2}$ a glass of red wine
salt and freshly ground
black pepper
some fresh herbs, such
as rosemary, sorrel,
marjoram, thyme…
$\frac{1}{2}$ a teaspoon of mace

Pre-heat the oven to medium.
Line a 2lb/1 kilo loaf tin with the
rashers of bacon. Leave the ends of
the rashers hanging down the
outside of the tin. Put in the fridge
until needed.

Mince the meat and liver together.
(A friendly butcher may do this
for you).

Put the minced meat and all the
remaining ingredients in a bowl and
mix well.

Cover with cling film and chill in a
fridge to allow the flavours to develop
for a couple of hours. Then take a
small quantity of mixture and fry it in
a small pan to check the seasoning -
there's nothing worse than a bland
terrine! Adjust the seasoning,
if necessary.

Put the meat mixture into the lined
loaf tin, press down firmly, and turn in
the ends of the bacon rashers to
wrap around what will be the base of
the terrine. Cover with foil.

Place the terrine into a deep roasting
tin containing enough boiling water to
come at least half way up the loaf tin.
Bake for approx 1 hour. The terrine
should just be pulling away from the
sides of the tin and the juices should
be dark red.

Leave the terrine in the water, still
covered, to cool. Chill in the fridge
overnight. Turn it out the next day;
the juices should have turned into a
delicious jelly.

Cut into chunky slices and serve with
fresh bread and some good chutney,
like Highfield's West Country
Chutney.

MEAT

131

'When we first came to the Mill we had no intention of it becoming a music venue, but I guess that it was inevitable given my background as a music promoter and as a professional in the arts. Music has always been an overwhelming passion of mine and the fact that two of our chefs have deep roots in the music business was the extra encouragement that I needed. Over the past three years many of the leading figures in contemporary folk, blues, country and jazz have appeared at the Mill and we now have the kind of reputation that gets agents calling us from America! The summer outdoor Courtyard Series is particularly magical and events can sell out months in advance. Another factor in the popularity of the music is that it's the only opportunity our visitors get to dine at the Mill in the evening. Almost everyone does before a show, and each evening has its own unique menu which compliments the night's music. Great food and great music has always been a really potent combination.'
*Bob Butler*

'Folks around here have been curious about our tour and what we thought of England. Invariably someone will ask Eddie or me about the food. We just smile and tell them about Otterton Mill… grinding the flour, freshly baked bread, gourmet meals and so on. They ask me what I ate and I have to say 'I don't know how to pronounce it, but it was heavenly.'
*Frank Thomas*

*Frank and Eddie Thomas are two brilliant bluesmen from Tupelo, Mississippi who played at the Mill in spring 2005.*

133

# OTTERTON SQUAB PIE

Enough to serve six

Heat the sunflower oil in a heavy-based pan and sauté the onions until they soften. Add the grated nutmeg, mace, cinnamon, cracked pepper and salt and continue to cook for a few minutes to release the flavours of the spices.

In a medium-sized glazed pie dish arrange layers of lamb, apples, prunes and the spiced onions, sprinkling each layer with a little dark brown sugar.

Pour on the meat stock.

Roll out the pastry to a size slightly larger than the pie dish. Lay the pastry over the dish, trim, seal and glaze with a little beaten egg or milk. Cover the pie crust with greaseproof paper (to stop it from browning too fast) and bake in a medium oven for about an hour. Remove the grease-proof and bake for a further 20 minutes to crisp up the crust. Serve hot with a good spoonful of clotted cream.

i

12oz/350g short-crust pastry
1lb 4oz/550g young Devon lamb, diced
2 medium onions, peeled and chopped
some sunflower oil
half a grated nutmeg
$\frac{1}{2}$ a teaspoon of mace
$\frac{1}{2}$ a teaspoon of cinnamon
sea salt and cracked black pepper
2lb/900g sharp dessert apples (such as Cox's), peeled cored and sliced
16 prunes
$\frac{1}{2}$ pint/300ml meat stock
some dark brown sugar
4oz/125g clotted cream

**134**

MEAT

*This is a traditional Devon dish which would originally have been made with squabs (young domesticated pigeons) as well as lamb. Prunes add a lovely sweet richness to the pie. Squab pie is traditionally served with clotted cream which, believe us, compliments it perfectly!*

# PORK, APPLE & CIDER CASSEROLE

Heat the oil in a flameproof casserole, or a heavy-based pan with a lid, and brown the meat. When it's browned, put the meat to one side. Using the same pan, add a little extra oil and soften the onion, garlic and celery. Sprinkle over any remaining seasoned flour and stir in. Then add the cider and let it bubble well. Return the meat to the pan and add the apples, fresh herbs and enough stock to cover it all.
Simmer until the meat is tender - about 1½ hours.
Season to taste - it's sometimes good to add a little sugar.
Serve with creamed potatoes.

*Variation: **Pork, Apple and Cider pie** make as above but with a little bit less cooking liquid. When the meat is cooked and tender place in a pie dish and cover with a pie crust, egg wash and bake in a hot oven for twenty minutes.*

Serves four to six

2 lbs/1kilo diced pork, tossed in seasoned flour
a little sunflower oil
2 medium-sized onions, peeled and chopped
2 to 4 cloves of garlic, peeled and crushed
4 sticks of celery - chopped
½ pint/300ml Jack Ratt's, or similar, local cider (see p100-101)
4 to 6 eating apples (preferably Cox's), cored and sliced
enough stock to cover
a small handful of mixed fresh herbs, chopped
sea salt and freshly ground black pepper

# RICH VENISON CASSEROLE WITH CHILLI CHOCOLATE

This is enough for eight people

Pre-heat oven to medium-low.
In a large heavy-based saucepan heat half the olive oil and fry the onions, garlic, leeks and celery for about 10 minutes until they've softened.
Remove and set aside on a plate.
Toss the meat in the seasoned flour until well coated.
Heat a further 2 tablespoons of the olive oil and fry the meat in small quantities until it is all well browned.
Remove each batch and set aside on a plate.

Return the meat and vegetables to the pan, add the chilli and then stir in the red wine, bring to the boil, add the stock, thyme, orange zest and seasonings. Transfer to a casserole with a tight-fitting lid, and bake slowly for $1\frac{1}{2}$ to 2 hours.
15 minutes before serving stir in the chilli chocolate.
Check and adjust the seasoning.
Serve.

5 lb/2 kilos venison, cubed
6-8 tablespoons of olive oil
3 large onions, peeled and chopped
6 cloves of garlic, peeled and crushed
4 leeks, washed and chopped
4 celery stalks, washed and chopped
3 tablespoons of wholemeal flour (seasoned with salt and black pepper)
half a bottle of red wine
1 pint/600ml of hot stock
a large bunch of fresh thyme
the zest of an orange
sea salt and freshly ground black pepper
2oz/50g chilli chocolate
$\frac{1}{4}$ chilli finely chopped

MEAT

First make a simple pesto. Strip the leaves from both bunches of basil. Put the leaves into a blender, along with the garlic and the grated cheddar, and season with a little salt and pepper. Blend; slowly adding oil, to make a stiff paste. Taste, and check the seasoning. Put into a bowl and set to one side.

Carefully remove the stalks from each mushroom and discard. Wipe the mushrooms with a clean cloth and put them in an oiled baking dish. Drizzle a little oil over the inside of each mushroom.
Put a heaped teaspoon of pesto into each mushroom and spread it over the surface. Sprinkle with cashews or walnuts and lightly press them in.
Place a mound of sweet potato mash on top, shaping it into a dome,
Add a basil leaf to each dome, then a round of cheese. (Or two rounds, for a large mushroom.)
Drizzle with a little more oil and then put into a medium oven for 20 to 30 minutes or until the mushrooms are cooked and the cheese is lightly browned.
Serve garnished with a few chives crossed on top.
Good with salad and some fresh crusty bread.

# AUTUMN STUFFED FIELD MUSHROOMS

Recently Jill found a crumpled recipe that she'd torn from a colour supplement years ago and adapted it to make this perfect autumnal dish. The recipe makes enough for four.

One very large, flat, field mushroom, or two medium-sized ones, per person
1lb/450g sweet potato, cooked, seasoned and mashed with butter and an egg.
4oz/125g of toasted cashews or walnuts
2 bunches of basil (put 8 leaves to one side)
2 cloves of garlic, peeled and crushed
4 to 6 tablespoons of olive oil
2oz/50g of grated cheddar cheese
6oz/175g soft mild goat's cheese (Vulscombe, or similar), sliced into rounds
sea salt and freshly ground black pepper
some chives to garnish

140

VEG

# MUSHROOM LOAF

Grease a 1lb/500g loaf tin generously with oil and coat it with breadcrumbs. Slice a couple of mushrooms and form them into a line (or some other decorative pattern) on the bottom of the tin. Chop the remaining mushrooms.

Heat the olive oil in a heavy-based large pan and sauté the onion and garlic until soft. Add the chopped mushrooms and fry for a further 2 to 3 minutes.

Put all the ingredients (except the egg, soy sauce and seasoning) into a food processor and give it a quick whiz. Then season to taste (you can taste the mix at this stage). Lastly add the egg. Give the mix a final quick whiz in the food processor. Don't overmix as the loaf should have some texture.

Spoon the mixture into tin. Bake in a medium oven for 45 minutes to 1 hour. Leave it in the tin until it's cool.

Serve either warm or cold. (It cuts better when cold.)

If cut into thin slices it makes a really good sandwich filling too.

(If you leave out the egg the loaf will still hold together reasonably well; it is then suitable for vegans.)

Freezes well.

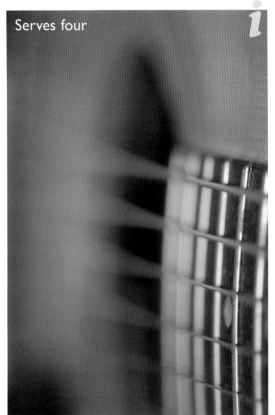

Serves four

1 onion, peeled and chopped
2 cloves of garlic, peeled and crushed
1lb/450g mushrooms
some olive oil
4oz/125g seeds (sunflower, sesame or pumpkin seeds - or a mixture), coarsely ground or chopped (to leave some texture)
8oz/225g fresh bread-crumbs (and some extra to coat the loaf tin)
2 tablespoons of fresh herbs, chopped
1 egg
some soy sauce
sea salt and freshly ground black pepper

VEG

# RAISED LEEK & RICE PIE

One 9 inch/22 cm spring-form tin, well oiled and floured.

In a fairly large bowl lightly beat the eggs. Add the rice, leeks, oil and cheese to the bowl. Season with two teaspoons of salt and plenty of pepper. Stir well, and set aside for 2 to 4 hours, giving the mixture a stir every now and then.

Heat the oven to a medium setting. Unfold the filo pastry sheets but keep them covered with a clean dry tea towel to prevent them drying out. Lightly brush the first sheet with olive oil and then lay it into the tin. Drape any edges down the outside of the tin. Repeat this with further sheets, brushing each with oil and laying it into the tin at an angle to the one below, making sure that the inner surface of the tin is covered.

Spoon the leek, rice and egg filling into the pie. Fold the edges of the sheets of filo back over the filling. Lay a couple more sheets on top and tuck them into the side of the tin. Brush each sheet with oil as you go. Bake for 40 or 50 minutes. Cover with foil if it looks as if the pastry is beginning to burn. Allow to cool for at least 10 minutes before turning out of the tin.

Good served with a homemade tomato sauce.
Four to six servings

1lb 8oz/700g leeks, washed, trimmed and finely shredded
4 large free range eggs
5oz/150g risotto rice (lightly pre-cooked with about $\frac{1}{2}$ cup of water/stock for a few minutes before using).
3 tablespoon olive oil - plus extra for brushing
7oz/200g sharp mature cheddar, grated
sea salt and fresh ground black pepper
about 8oz/225g filo pastry

# LEEK, WALNUT & BLUE CHEESE TART

Melt the butter in a heavy-based pan and sauté leeks for about 20 minutes. Arrange the cooked leeks and the chopped walnuts in the pastry case. Mix the eggs and the double cream together and season with salt, pepper and nutmeg.

Pour into the tart and crumble the blue cheese over the top.

Bake in a moderate oven for 25 to 30 minutes until the eggs are set but the tart is still slightly wobbly in the centre.

Basic tart crust, blind baked (see p20)
3 large leeks diagonally cut into $\frac{1}{2}$ inch/1 cm sections
4oz/125g butter
4oz/125g toasted walnuts, chopped
$\frac{1}{2}$ pint/300ml double cream
2 eggs plus an extra egg yolk
sea salt and freshly ground black pepper
fresh nutmeg
3oz/75g ripe Devon Blue cheese

VEG

# SPICY PUY LENTIL SALAD

Put the lentils into a saucepan with plenty of salted water; bring to the boil and then cook gently until 'al dente'. (Don't overcook - you don't want a mush).

Heat the oil and sauté the onion and garlic until soft. Add the cumin, coriander and turmeric and cook for a further few minutes to draw out the flavour of the spices. When the lentils are cooked and drained, but still warm, add them to the spicy onion and tip into a bowl. Season to taste. Add more oil, if needed, and a splash of wine vinegar. Stir in a good quantity of fresh chopped coriander leaves.

The same simple spicy mixture can be stirred into cooked brown, or white rice. Add some raisins and toasted, flaked almonds. Chopped mixed peppers add colour to both salads.

# LEMON & HONEY DRESSING

Shake everything together well in a lidded jar.

*i*  8oz/225g puy lentils
1 onion, peeled and chopped
2 or 3 cloves of garlic, peeled and crushed
$1\frac{1}{2}$ to 2 dessertspoons of sunflower oil
1 tablespoon of freshly ground coriander
1 tablespoon of freshly ground cumin
1 dessertspoon of turmeric
a large handful of fresh coriander, chopped

*i*  the juice of 1 lemon
1 tablespoon of runny honey
double the quantity of sunflower oil to lemon juice
seasoning to taste.

SALAD

# FIRE SALAD

Julienne slice (into long, matchstick-sized, narrow strips) the carrots, courgettes and red, green and yellow peppers.
Mix in a bowl with lemon and honey dressing and enough toasted sesame seeds to evenly cover the vegetables.

*i* Equal quantities of:
carrots
courgettes (or cucumber depending on the season)
red, green and yellow peppers
1oz/25g toasted sesame seeds
small handful of coriander leaves

# CELERY, APRICOT & WALNUT SALAD

Mix all the ingredients together in a bowl.
Dress with equal amounts of mayonnaise and crème fraiche and season with black pepper.
This is also really good dressed with lemon and honey.

*i* 3oz/75g of chopped and toasted walnuts
a head of celery, washed, trimmed and sliced finely on the diagonal
4oz/125g of moist, pre-soaked dried apricots, quartered

# DEVILS CAULDRON (CHOCOLATE APPLE CAKE)

Grease or line a 9 inch cake tin.

In a food processor whiz together the sugar and the eggs until they're smooth and creamy.
Add the flour, salt and cinnamon and lightly mix them in.
Dissolve the bicarbonate in the lemon juice (it will fizz) and add it to the cake mixture. Mix lightly in.
Pour the mixture into a large bowl. Use the processor to thinly slice the apples. Then stir the apples into the mixture.
Pour into the prepared cake tin and bake for about 45 minutes in a medium oven, until the top is springy and a skewer inserted comes out clean.
Make the glaze a few minutes before the cake is ready by melting the butter with the other ingredients to make a smooth rich chocolate sauce.
Add a small amount of chilli at first (chilli powder does vary in strength) and check, add more chilli to taste; it should have a bite to it.
Allow the sauce to just come to the boil and then remove it from the heat. For an extra chocolatey sauce drop in some squares of very dark chocolate and let them melt into the sauce.
Prick the hot cake in a number of places with a wooden skewer and pour over the hot chocolate. Leave to cool before cutting.

A delicious, wonderfully sticky cake; it makes a great pudding served with clotted cream. This recipe will give you a large cake that will serve about ten people.

12oz/350g cooking apples, peeled and cored
3 eggs
8oz/225g light or dark muscovado sugar
4oz/125g plain unbleached white or wholemeal flour
$\frac{1}{2}$ teaspoon of salt
1 level teaspoon of cinnamon 1 teaspoon of bicarbonate of soda
$1\frac{1}{2}$ teaspoons of fresh lemon juice

CHOCOLATE GLAZE
2oz/50g butter (unsalted is best, but either will do)
2 tablespoons of milk
2oz/50g sifted icing sugar
2 tablespoons of good quality cocoa
a good pinch of chilli powder
some squares of dark chocolate (70% cocoa solids) - optional

146

# OPEN FACED PEAR & ALMOND TART

Arrange the sliced pears attractively in the baked pastry case. (If they are not quite ripe enough lightly poach the pear slices in apple juice and drain).

Beat together the egg, sugar, butter, flour, almond essence, ground almonds and cream.

Spread the egg and almond mix over the pears and then scatter the flaked almonds over the top.

Bake in a moderate oven for 20 to 30 minutes until the mix has set and is a light golden brown.

*i*

9 inch/22cm sweet pastry case (see p40)
4 large ripe Commice or Conference pears, peeled, cored and sliced
3oz/75g ground almonds
2oz/50g toasted flaked almonds
3oz/75g soft butter
3oz/75g golden caster sugar
$\frac{1}{2}$ teaspoon of almond essence
1 tablespoon of plain flour
1 egg
1 tablespoon of double cream

# DEVON HONEY BREAD AND BUTTER PUDDING

Preheat the oven to medium 15 minutes before you are ready to cook the pudding.
Butter a medium-sized oven proof dish.

Cut the crusts off the loaf and cut into medium-thick slices.
Butter the slices and spread them with honey. (Don't spread all the slices at once, just in case you don't use the whole loaf; you can spread more as you go along).
Butter a medium-sized ovenproof dish. Cover the bottom with a layer of bread slices. Sprinkle with raisins, chopped dates, and lemon zest. Continue to layer the bread and fruit until the dish is full, finishing with a layer of bread.
Beat the eggs with the cream and pour it over the pudding, pressing the slices down lightly. Leave to rest in a cool place for the liquid to be absorbed into the bread - about 30 minutes.  If necessary add a little more milk or cream before cooking.
Before cooking sprinkle with brown sugar and grated nutmeg to taste. Bake in the oven for about 30 minutes or until the pudding is lightly firm to touch and crispy on top.
Serve warm with clotted cream.

*A rich, indulgent pudding to have as a treat on a cold autumn day*

a large loaf of good white bread (Otterton Mill bread is the best!)
some butter
some Devon honey
4oz/125g of raisins or chopped dates
the zest of 2 lemons
2 eggs
$\frac{1}{2}$ pint/300ml of double cream
some grated nutmeg
a handful of soft brown sugar

## Our organic drink people: Gabriel and Caroline David at Luscombe Farm.

Like so many of Devon's loveliest places, Luscombe Farm is well tucked away; in this case at the end of a narrow meandering lane that tracks the course of the Dart as it tumbles southwards. The grey stone farmhouse exudes a powerful sense of belonging, as though it has been there as long as the river itself. Gabriel David's parents live in it; he and his wife Caroline live in a converted farm building at the rear. As we stand talking in the yard, the peace is disturbed by the bleeping of a reversing fork-lift. 'The price of success,' Gabriel says, doing his best to sound rueful.

(Oddly enough, we had been talking about horse-shoe bats. 'The cattle eat our apple-pulp, dung-beetles live on the result, and the horse-shoe bats live on the beetles. It's a nice cycle.')

When the Davids moved to Luscombe, it had, like innumerable West Country farms, a fairly rudimentary cider-making set-up. 'We wanted to keep it going,' Gabriel says, 'partly because there was a serious risk of local orchards being entirely lost. These were growing lovely old varieties of apple, like Quench, Tale Sweet, Pig's Snout and Slack ma Girdle, which are heading for extinction because the market for them has almost disappeared. But we soon realised that making real cider was a pretty chancy way to make a living no matter how good it is.'

(And, incidentally, Luscombe cider is very good; it was the National Taste Awards Cider of the Year in 2000.)

So in 1997 the Davids went whole-heartedly organic and started producing entirely additive-free apple juice and apple juice blends: apple and apricot, apple and ginger, apple and pear, apple and elderflower. Then ginger beer.

'That came about because the nearest pub from here involves a drive. Not an easy one, either. Which means that after your first pint you have to switch to something non-alcoholic. And I got sick to death of lime and lemonade. So I thought of ginger beer, which has a nice legal kick to it.'

Luscombe makes two varieties of ginger beer, using wonderfully juicy Brazilian root ginger. The 'Cool' one leaves a light sting on the palate; the 'Hot' one gives you a real zap. (Ideal if you've just walked up the Otter to the Mill on a cold day and want something to quench your thirst and heat you up at the same time.) Luscombe also makes what is probably the best lemonade in the world. That came about because Gabriel spent four years of his childhood in Sicily and remembered the deliciousness of the local home-made version. Which is why he imports organic juice from Palermo to make Luscombe's celebrated Sicilian Lemonade.

The Luscombe production line is housed in a converted milking parlour. It's like entering the Tardis; inside an ancient stone, timber and slate structure there's a sleek, hygienic, high-tech world populated by people in white overalls and hairnets. Gabriel is rightly proud of the fact that the building hasn't been irreversibly interfered with. 'The walls, the ceilings, everything, have been built within the original structure. We could dismantle it all and take it out and the place would be more or less as we found it. I like to think that in a hundred or two hundred years this farm, this building, will still be here, unharmed by us.'

And with a good deal of luck and dung-beetles, the horse-shoe bats will still be there too.

Ed is the Mill's latest recruit. Actually a drama graduate, Ed learned most of what he knows working for Conran at the Bibendum and Bluebird restaurants in London before taking on his own establishment in Hammersmith. Originally from farming stock, he eventually found the lure of the countryside too strong to resist, and he 'escaped' to Devon recently, and lives in the beautiful farm at Harcombe that has now become his family home.

Jill's mum was a really great post-War plain cook. She made fantastic steak and kidney pie and shepherd's pie and roast dinners. She made wonderful cakes. But she wouldn't try new things. Garlic and herbs? No chance… So she gave Jill all the basic skills and a mad desire to try everything and experiment.

Self-taught cooks like Jill are often amongst the best; they tend to be more intuitive and instinctive and are almost always passionate about food. 'Food should burst with colour,' she says. 'First you eat with your eyes, and then if it tastes good too - that's brilliant!' Jill ran the Arnolfini restaurant in Bristol for several years before finding her way to the mill.

*Jill Adams*
*Head Chef*

*Ed Chester*

STAFF

Ian is an exceptional fellow. He grew up in west London and got bitten by the emerging sixties R'n'B music boom and decided that more than anything he wanted to be a professional musician. So he became one. His chosen instrument was the blues harmonica and over the years he's played with just about everyone. Later he indulged his other passion, food, and he taught himself to be one heck of a great chef too. With his son he started Harpoon Louis, a now infamous bar, restaurant and music venue in Taunton before moving to Otterton Mill as a chef. Ian still plays the blues regularly with his band the Supervampers and he's also in great demand as a sit-in musician at the Mill's Thursday Night sessions.

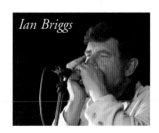

Ian Briggs

'Having been a bit of a rock chick and led a rock & roll life during the 80s, it was time to get into some serious work and earn myself some money, and cooking had always got my creative juices flowing. In 2000 I got bitten by wanderlust and found myself in the Caribbean, cooking on boats and anywhere else that would have me. Three years later I started working at the Mill and love their style and approach to food.'

Sarah is another self-taught cook. She started her professional life with an outside catering business she ran with a friend. It worked really well despite the fact that neither of them could drive.

Passionate about food, she's always dipped in and out of professional cooking.

'It's a very creative process. I need to be experimental. If I use a recipe I read it through, grasp the basic idea, and then extemporize a bit. Apart from anything else, it takes so much longer if you have to keep referring back to the recipe.'

Sarah Cousins

INDEX

INDEX

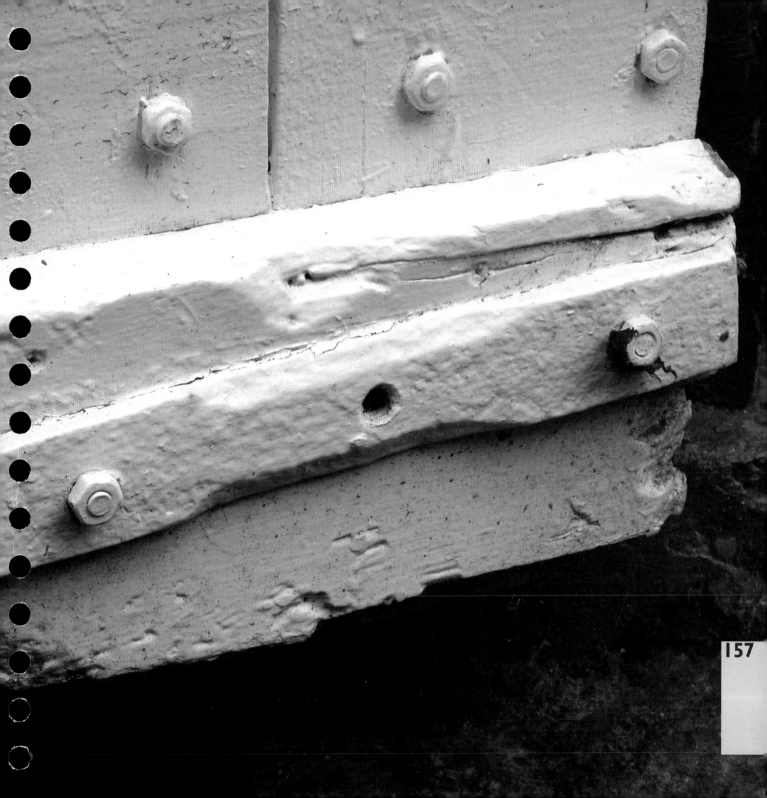

157

## WRITERS, PHOTOGRAPHERS, DESIGNER

**Mal Peet** and **Elspeth Graham** have been writing books together for as many years as they've been regulars at Otterton Mill. Nowadays Mal mainly writes long novels for young adults, while Elspeth mainly writes short non-fiction books for younger children. They worked together again on the Otterton Mill book - they love everything about the place, the buildings, the river, the walks, the atmosphere and, not least, the food!

**Piers Rawson** is a documentary and landscape photographer living on the borders between Somerset, Dorset and Devon. www.scenae.dircon.co.uk

**Pauline Rook** is a photgrapher of people, particularly those involved in matters rural. She draws her inspiration from the richness of the local landscape, architecture and the people themselves. www.rookphoto.co.uk

**Kimberly Rainford** is based in Exmouth, Devon. Her images are tactile, inviting and refreshing. She has an interestingly different approach to food photography (like balancing beetroot on a beam, without breathing). www.kimberlyrainford.co.uk

**Tony Weaver** is an Exeter based designer who comes from a sculpture background. This may explain his creative, imaginative and sometimes irreverent attitude to image and text.

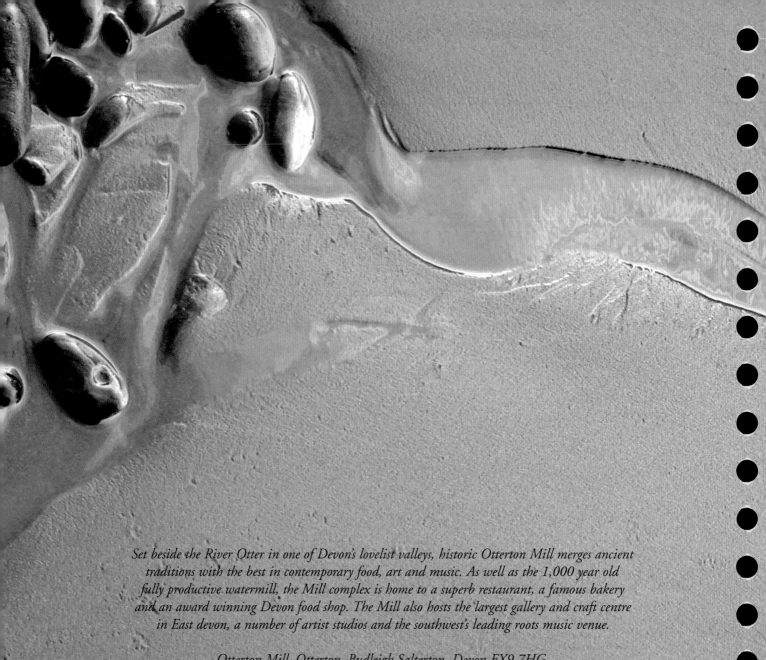

Set beside the River Otter in one of Devon's lovelist valleys, historic Otterton Mill merges ancient traditions with the best in contemporary food, art and music. As well as the 1,000 year old fully productive watermill, the Mill complex is home to a superb restaurant, a famous bakery and an award winning Devon food shop. The Mill also hosts the largest gallery and craft centre in East devon, a number of artist studios and the southwest's leading roots music venue.

Otterton Mill, Otterton, Budleigh Salterton, Devon EX9 7HG.

Tel: 01395 568521
escape@ottertonmill.com
www.ottertonmill.com